Dedication

To my husband, Mark, who supported me and put up with the messy kitchen and piles of books on the dining room table. And special thanks to my mother, Ferol Smith Golden, and friend Karen Kast, who helped kitchen test recipes. Finally, thanks to all the family and friends who tasted and gave such helpful feedback.

Contents

Introduction

Most people discover fajitas and the delicious side dishes, garnishes, and condiments that go with them in restaurants and believe that they're too difficult and time-consuming to make at home. Actually, fajita dinners are quick and easy to prepare; in fact, they're perfect for cooks with busy schedules.

Cutting and marinating the meat the night before or earlier in the day lets you cook a dinner for two—or for many— even after a busy workday. You can prepare all the side dishes, garnishes, and condiments ahead of time as well, so the final cooking process takes less than thirty minutes. And you can speed up the preparation even more by purchasing bottled salsas, prepared guacamole, and canned refried beans.

You'll discover that fajitas are great for entertaining—your guests can have fun selecting their own delicious combinations from a fajita buffet. And learning to prepare them is a great way to introduce yourself to southwestern cuisine.

What Are Fajitas?

Fajitas are really just a jazzed-up version of an old cowboy snack—grilled meat wrapped in a flour tortilla. They originated in the Texas region of the American Southwest. The word *fajita* ("little belt" in Spanish) refers to beef skirt steak, a tough but flavorful cut that traditionally is marinated and grilled over an open mesquite fire. The modern versions of fajitas evolved from several traditional recipes that have influenced cooks throughout much of the Southwest. Tacos al carbon, charolitas, and carnitas are all dishes in which grilled beef or pork is served in soft or fried tortillas with a variety of condiments.

Modern fajitas have evolved to include beef, pork, poultry, and even shrimp as their main ingredient, accompanied by grilled or sautéed vegetables and all sorts of condiments. Toppings and side dishes include tomatoes, tomatillos, chile sauces, fresh cilantro, beans, rice, guacamole, and sour cream. Vegetarian fajitas can be made with beans, cheese, or vegetables instead of meat as their main ingredient.

The History of Southwestern Cuisine

The American Southwest is loosely defined as the region encompassing New Mexico, Arizona, Texas, southern Colorado, and southern California. Southwestern cuisine reflects the diversity of both the terrain and the people who settled it. The corn, beans, squash, nuts, and game on which southwestern cuisine is based originated with the local Native American Indians. When the Spaniards and other Europeans came they brought wheat, rice, fruit, onions, garlic, and grapes. From Mexico came chiles, tomatoes, avocados, and chocolate. The cowboys who tended cattle and other ranch animals developed their own traditional ways of cooking: barbecuing and stewing. All these foods and cooking methods came together to form a unique and harmonious blend.

Southwestern cuisine might not be considered sophisticated, but it is undeniably tasty, elegant, and easy to prepare. Perhaps that explains why it's become increasingly more popular and more mainstream—along with its cousin, "Tex-Mex" cuisine—while other ethnic or regional foods have waxed and waned in popularity. From fine restaurants to fast-food chains, you'll find southwestern dishes such as fajitas on menus all across the nation.

The Essence of Balance

One of the real attractions of southwestern cuisine is that it is balanced, both in nutrition and flavor. Nutritionally, southwestern foods work wonders with simple ingredients. Staples such as rice, beans, tortillas, corn, and nuts are all sources of different types of protein; used together, they provide a healthy combination of proteins. Salsas and relishes incorporate many nutritious vegetables. Cheeses, often used as an accent, provide calcium, protein, and other nutrients.

And then there's the balance of flavors. The Southwest is a region where the sun always shines, the temperatures soar, and the chiles grow very hot. Recipes feature foods spiked with freshly chopped or roasted chiles, cayenne pepper, or chile sauces, but their constant heat is offset by ingredients with a cooling effect. Foods that are rich (such as butter, cheese, sour cream, and avocados), acidic (citrus juices, tomatoes, and vinegar), and starchy (rice, beans, and tortillas) all help soothe the palate and balance the effect of the hot spices. Many southwestern dishes feature well-chosen combinations of hot and cool ingredients, and hot and spicy dishes on the menu are usually accompanied by cooler ones.

About the Recipes...

Most of the recipes I've included in this book focus on fajitas and variations on that theme. There are also many recipes for foods to serve with fajitas, so you can create your own full-scale southwestern feasts. Some of the recipes for side dishes and condiments are traditional; others are my own adaptations of classic dishes. Once you know the secrets of spicing, marinating, and cooking fajitas, you'll be able to expand your repertoire to include all kinds of southwestern dishes.

One note on using the recipes: As a cooking teacher I've always encouraged experimentation. I rarely prepare recipes exactly as they're printed; instead, I add a dash more of this or that to tailor each recipe to my personal taste. The recipes I've included in this book should work well just as they're written, but consider the amount of seasonings (chiles, herbs, and spices) as mere guidelines, and vary them according to your own preference. Taste is as subjective as the appreciation of art; I love cilantro and lots of hot chiles, but you might not. So feel free to use more or less of any seasoning. The same philosophy applies to the use of condiments—serve a variety of salsas, relishes, and sauces at mealtime to encourage everyone to flavor their food to their own taste. Once you've got the feel for southwestern cuisine, try inventing whole new recipes or combinations of dishes.

Before you plunge into the recipes in this book, I suggest you browse through the following section on ingredients used in southwestern cookery. The more familiar you are with the spices and other ingredients, the more successful you'll be in adding your own creative touch to my recipes.

Lisa Golden Schroeder

The Southwestern Pantry

Some of the ingredients used in authentic southwestern cooking might be unfamiliar to you, but don't worry—you'll find that most of what you need is readily available. You can buy all the basic ingredients—such as tomatoes, onions, garlic, citrus fruits, corn, bell peppers, rices, and winter and summer squashes—in any well-stocked grocery store.

If you can't find an ingredient in your local supermarket, try food co-ops, Hispanic markets, or even Oriental markets, which usually carry fresh cilantro (known as Chinese parsley) and a wide assortment of fresh, dried, and ground chiles. Mail-order companies (page 140) are another easy and convenient source of seasonings, salsas, fresh chiles, and canned produce.

Fresh Fruits and Vegetables

Avocado

This popular fruit, known for its leathery skin, pale green flesh, and large pit, is sold in almost all grocery stores. The best avocados are the nutty-flavored Hass avocados from California; look for their dark (almost black), bumpy skin. Florida avocados, which have a thinner, smoother skin, are not nearly as flavorful or as silky in texture. To ensure proper ripening buy avocados a few days before you want to use them. Place them in a closed paper sack, unrefrigerated, to speed ripening. Avocados are the main ingredient in guacamole.

Jicama

This popular Mexican root vegetable resembles a large brown turnip. Its flesh has a nutty, slightly sweet taste and a crisp texture that some compare to that of water chestnuts. It is most often served in salads or as a dipper for salsas or guacamole. Occasionally it is lightly stir-fried and served as a vegetable side dish. Jicamas should be very firm, with a smooth, unblemished skin. Smaller jicamas are best, since the larger ones tend to be woody. Just peel off the brown skin with a sharp paring knife before you cut up the vegetable.

Nopales

Nopales are the flat green pads from the prickly pear cactus. They have a flavor similar to that of green string beans and are used in salads, with eggs, and in soups. Canned nopales are most common, though you can sometimes find them fresh in southwestern or Mexican markets. Fresh nopales must be peeled and blanched before use. *Nopalitos* are cut-up nopales used in cooking.

Mangoes, Papayas, Pineapples

These tropical fruits are popular in southwestern relishes, salads, sauces, and desserts.

Mangoes—Mangoes are picked green, but should be ripened at room temperature until they are yellowish-orange with a rosy spot on one end. Peel the skin with a paring knife or vegetable peeler. Slice wedges lengthwise from the large, almond-shaped pit.

Papayas—Papayas are picked green. Ripen them at room temperature until they are deep yellow, with minimal green at the stem end. Peel the skin with a paring knife. The small black seeds can be either scooped out or eaten.

Pineapples—Pineapples are picked ripe; the shell color is *not* an indicator of ripeness. Look for fruit that smell sweet, have fresh green leaves, and contain no soft spots. Twist or cut off the crown of leaves. Peel the skin with a sharp knife. Cut the fruit in wedges and remove the fibrous center core, if desired.

Plantains

Plantains are related to bananas, but are larger and usually have a deeper yellow flesh. Cooked unripe plantains taste like potatoes and are served as a vegetable. They are sweeter if allowed to ripen completely, until their skin becomes black.

Pomegranates

This large red fruit grows on trees in Arizona and California and is sold in grocery stores throughout the country. You simply break or cut open the heavy skin to reveal the fruit, which consists of small, deep pink, tart-sweet seeds. The seeds are used to garnish salads and desserts.

Tomatillos Resembling small green tomatoes—but not to be confused with unripe red tomatoes—tomatillos are enclosed in papery husks. Their flavor is very tart, with a hint of sweetness. Tomatillos are used primarily in sauces, either fresh or cooked, and sometimes in salads. Before using tomatillos, peel off their husks and rinse off the sticky residue. Canned tomatillos are available in Hispanic markets and the Mexican foods sections of well-stocked supermarkets.

Nuts and Seeds

Almonds Almonds are the preferred nut in Spanish-inspired sauces, fillings, and desserts.

Pecans The largest pecan orchards in the United States are in the Southwest, where pecans are used extensively in salads, rice, fillings, sweets, and other foods.

Pine Nuts (Piñons, Pignolis)

These small, oval, cream-colored nuts come from pine trees that grow in the deserts of the Southwest. The nuts are gathered by hand, which makes them expensive, but there's no substitute for their rich flavor in desserts, fillings, or rice dishes. Many of the pine nuts sold in the United States come from China and are longer and more slender than the native variety. Buy pine nuts in small quantities at co-ops or stores with a fast turnover; their high fat content causes them to turn rancid quickly unless they are stored in a cool, dry place.

Pumpkin Seeds (Pepitas)

Pepitas are the hulled green-colored seeds from pumpkins. They are used in sauces and as a garnish for soups and salads. Buy them raw in health food stores or co-ops.

Toasting Nuts

Toasting enhances the flavor of nuts. Just place the nuts in a shallow ungreased pan and bake at 350°F, stirring and checking them frequently. When done they'll be lightly browned and fragrant. Almonds and pecans take 7 to 12 minutes; pine nuts take 5 to 7 minutes. You can also toast nuts by stirring them in an ungreased skillet over medium heat until they are done.

Cheeses

Aged Goat Cheese, Parmesan, and Asiago
These cheeses have sharp flavors and are good accents for topping salads, chili, beans, and baked dishes. They can also be used as substitutes for Cotija, an aged Mexican cheese.

Asadero
Asadero is a white Mexican cheese that is similar to Mozzarella but has a tangier, more buttery flavor. It is usually shaped into balls or logs. Asadero is used for melting and can be found in Mexican or southwestern markets.

Cheddar, Colby, and Longhorn
The mild Longhorn and Colby Cheddars are popular in the Southwest. They melt well for making cheese crisps and topping baked tortilla dishes. Sharp Cheddars are shredded for tacos, salads, and melting.

Chihuahua Cheese
A Mexican cheese similar to Longhorn Cheddar, Chihuahua cheese melts well and becomes stringy like Mozzarella. You will find it in Mexican or southwestern markets.

Co-Jack
A mixture of mild Cheddar and Monterey Jack cheeses. Co-Jack can be used as a substitute in any recipe that calls for Colby and/or Monterey Jack.

Cotija (Queso Seco)
An aged, low-moisture cheese with a sharp flavor, Cotija is used crumbled on top of dishes. Aged goat cheese, Parmesan, or Asiago can be substituted. You will find Cotija in Mexican or southwestern markets.

Fresh Goat Cheeses
Soft, mild goat cheeses are a wonderful complement to beans and chiles and are used in fillings or to garnish southwestern dishes. They are available in most grocery stores.

Monterey Jack
A white, semi-soft cheese from California, Monterey Jack is as popular for southwestern dishes as the Cheddars. It has a mild flavor that melts well. An aged, "dry" Jack is also available and has a sharper, more complex flavor.

Queso Fresco (Fresh Cheese)
A white Mexican cheese, Queso Fresco is similar in texture and flavor to a salty Farmer cheese. Queso Fresco is used in salads, tacos, and enchiladas and sprinkled on hot beans, but it gets rubbery when broiled. Feta cheese can be used as a substitute. Look for Queso Fresco in Mexican and southwestern markets.

Herbs and Spices

Achiote (Annatto) These brick-red seeds are from the tropical annatto tree, which grows on Mexico's Yucatan Peninsula. The seeds must be soaked in water to soften them, then puréed into a paste. The flavor is subtle—slightly acidic and reminiscent of green olives. Achiote colors fish, poultry, and pork a deep red.

Anise Seed Anise is a distinctly flavored spice most often used to add a licorice flavor to pastries and syrups. It is similar in flavor to fennel seed.

Chili Powder

Chili powder with an *i* refers not to chile peppers but to a seasoning blend of ground red chiles, oregano, cumin, and garlic. Chili powder is generally used to season the dish of the same name (spelled the same way). I prefer to make my own chili powder blend, but Gebhardt's from San Antonio is a good commercial brand.

Ingredients

¼ cup ground red chile (mild, medium, or hot)

1 tablespoon cumin seeds, toasted and ground

*1 teaspoon **each** ground cloves, ground coriander, oregano leaves, and garlic salt*

Directions

Mix all ingredients well; store tightly covered away from light and heat. Use to flavor stews, meat mixtures, or marinades.

Makes about ⅓ cup

>><<<<<<<<<<<<<<<<<<<<<<<<<<<<<<<<<<<<<<<<<<<<

Cilantro (Coriander, Chinese Parsley, Mexican Parsley)

Some consider cilantro, an herb with lacy green leaves, to be the secret ingredient for a wide variety of southwestern marinades and dishes—it's certainly essential for fajitas. And some consider its pungent, woodsy, citrus flavor an acquired taste (dried cilantro has virtually no flavor compared to fresh). Fresh cilantro is now widely available in supermarkets, but try Hispanic, Oriental, or farmers' markets for large, fresh bunches. Look for glossy green bunches, with no yellow or slimy leaves. Cilantro will keep up to a week if refrigerated with the stems in water and the top covered with plastic wrap. The seeds of the fresh cilantro plant are called coriander seeds.

Fresh Sonoran Seasoning

Ingredients

5 tablespoons chopped fresh cilantro leaves

3 tablespoons chopped fresh oregano leaves

2 tablespoons chopped fresh thyme leaves

*1 tablespoon **each** ground red chile,* ground black pepper, and ground cumin*

1 small fresh jalapeño chile, stemmed

2 cloves garlic

Directions

Place all ingredients in food processor. Process until finely chopped.

Makes about 1 cup

*Use mild, medium, or hot red chile, or make a blend that will produce the level of spiciness you desire.

Cinnamon Available in both stick and ground forms, cinnamon is popular in desserts as well as in savory dishes of Spanish and Mexican influence (stews, beans, and rice). Use stick cinnamon to flavor beverages and syrups or grind it for a strong cinnamon flavor.

Coriander Seed Coriander is the seed of the cilantro plant (cilantro is also sometimes called coriander). The flavor of the seed is different from that of the plant and much more subtle. Usually used ground, coriander seeds have a sweetness that is well suited to desserts, salad dressings (especially for fruits), and stews. It is used whole for pickling or poaching fruits.

Cumin

Cumin Cumin, available either ground or as seeds, is the predominant spice in southwestern and Mexican cooking. The flavor of freshly ground cumin seeds cannot be duplicated in store-bought ground cumin, since the oils that flavor it are quite volatile. Toast the seeds first in a small skillet over medium heat, shaking the pan often, until they are fragrant (about 3 minutes). Grind them in a mortar and pestle, spice grinder, or clean coffee grinder.

Epazote

Epazote A pungent, medicinal-tasting herb with pointed, serrated leaves, epazote originates in the Yucatan Peninsula of Mexico. Fresh epazote is hard to find in American markets but easy to grow yourself. Dried epazote is available, but its flavor pales in comparison to fresh. Epazote is delicious in soups and fillings, but is used most often with black beans (some claim it reduces the flatulence-causing sugars in beans).

Mint (Yerba Buena)

Mint (Yerba Buena) Mint grows well in the heat of the desert Southwest. It is used in salads, vegetables, beans, desserts, and sun tea. Wild mint is gathered in rural areas for medicinal teas. Buy it fresh at the grocery store—dried mint has a dull flavor.

Oregano (Mexican or Greek)

A natural with tomatoes, meats, beans, and vegetables, oregano is second in popularity only to cilantro for southwestern cooking. You can use it either fresh or dried, but you need only one-third the amount of dried to match the flavor of fresh. Mexican and Greek oregano have a stronger flavor than Italian oregano. You will find oregano anywhere fresh herbs are sold.

Rosemary

Rosemary Hedges of this Mediterranean herb grow profusely throughout the Southwest. The leaves are long, narrow, and dark green, resembling pine needles, attached to a heavy branch. Rosemary's heady aroma makes it a favorite for roasting or grilling meats. Chop fresh leaves for use in marinades or with potatoes. Dried leaves are equally fragrant if they are crushed before use.

>><<<<<<<<<<<<<<<<<<<<<<<<<<<<<<<<<<<<<<<<<<<<<<<<<<<<<

Pantry Staples

Beans, Dried or Canned (Pinto, Black, Red Kidney, Garbanzo)

An inexpensive and filling form of protein, beans (*frijoles*) have long been a staple of Mexican and American Indian diets. Spotted pinto beans are the favored variety, used in soups, stews, and burritos and served refried as a side dish (*refrito*). Black beans (*frijoles negros* or turtle beans) are richer in flavor and originate from the Yucatan Peninsula and central Mexico. Garbanzos (chickpeas) came to the region from Spain and are popular served as a side dish or in soups and salads. Dried beans benefit from soaking prior to cooking; soaking shortens their cooking time and, some cooks feel, improves their digestibility. Health food stores, co-ops, and Hispanic markets are good sources of fresh dried beans. Good quality canned beans have the advantage of convenience, since they are already cooked; be sure to rinse them well before using them.

Chocolate

Used in beverages and desserts, chocolate is as popular in the Southwest as it is in Mexico. Mexican chocolate bars from Oaxaca are flavored with cinnamon, sugar, and ground almonds.

Chorizo

A spicy, Spanish-style sausage, chorizo is usually made from pork. It is crumbled, browned, and then served with beans and eggs or used as a filling for various tortilla dishes. Chorizo seasoning is delicious and really has no substitute—you can use hot Italian sausage, but the flavor is quite different. If you want to keep some chorizo on hand, store it in the freezer.

Corn Husks

Dried corn husks are the traditional wrapping for tamales. Either fresh husks (with the corn silk removed) or dried husks can be used to form "boats" to hold sautéed vegetable mixtures. Soak the husks in water to keep them pliable, and tie the ends together with kitchen twine to shape each boat.

Lard

Before refrigeration, lard was the only cooking fat available in the Southwest. Most cooks now use butter, margarine, or vegetable oils (olive oil, in particular). Lard, which is traditionally rendered from pork fat, lends a distinctive flavor to beans, pie crusts, and tortillas.

Masa Harina
The Quaker Oats Company produces a widely distributed masa harina; it is a dehydrated yellow corn flour made from dried corn kernels that have been softened in a lime solution (calcium hydroxide), then finely ground. It is easily made into *masa,* the corn dough used for tortillas and tamales. Do not substitute cornmeal, which is much coarser. Blue cornmeal masa can be ordered from New Mexico. Other brands of masa are available in co-ops and southwestern markets.

Tequila
Tequila is a clear liquor distilled from the agave cactus (century plant) that grows in the southwestern desert. Use tequila in beverages, sauces, and marinades for meats.

Tortillas
Tortillas are round, unleavened breads made from either corn or wheat flour; they are the staple bread of the Southwest. Both types are widely available in supermarkets, but don't miss trying fresh homemade tortillas, which you can make yourself. Tortillas are served warm to accompany meals, used as an integral part of many dishes, or cut and fried to make chips for snacking. Flour tortillas are the traditional partner for fajitas and are the most popular kind of tortilla in Arizona and southern California. Corn tortillas are more common in New Mexico. Both types are used in Texas.

Cooking Equipment

Once you start to get better acquainted with southwestern cooking, you might want to consider purchasing one or more of the following utensils. They are all useful pieces of equipment frequently used in southwestern cooking. None are essential, but they are all nice to have and can make cooking much easier.

Cast-Iron Fajita Skillet
An oblong or round skillet used to broil meat, a fajita skillet can be preheated in the oven and used to serve sizzling-hot meat and vegetables at the table. Meat can also be broiled directly on it.

Tortilla Press
The masa corn dough used to make corn tortillas can be difficult to roll out, and a tortilla press makes the job much easier. A press is not necessary for flour tortillas.

Mortar and Pestle or Spice Grinder

A mortar and pestle, a spice grinder, or even a clean coffee-bean grinder is indispensable for making freshly ground red chile powder or grinding toasted cumin seeds.

Comal

This round, cast-iron skillet from Mexico is used to bake and reheat tortillas.

Grill Basket

This flat metal basket with a long handle holds shrimp, strips of meat, or individual vegetables on a grill; it makes turning and removing them easier.

Long-Handled Grilling Tools

Long-handled forks and spatulas are used to turn and move meat and vegetables on the grill. A fork is also handy for roasting chiles over an open flame. A long basting brush is used to baste meat or vegetables on the grill. Long tongs are indispensable for handling grilled foods or coals.

Spritz Bottle

Fill a small hand sprayer with water and always have it on hand to put out flare-ups when grilling.

Metal or Bamboo Skewers

Skewers hold meats or vegetables on the grill. Bamboo skewers need to be soaked in water for about 20 minutes before use to prevent burning.

A Guide to Chiles

Many different varieties of hot chiles are grown and used throughout the Southwest. Substituting one type of chile for another might subtly alter the flavor of a dish; as you become more familiar with different chiles, you'll become more adept at altering recipes. To avoid confusion I refer to all chiles, both fresh and dried, as *chiles*. Chili ending with an *i* refers to a seasoning blend flavored with ground red chiles, and also to the main dish that is made with chili powder. Many chiles are used before they are fully ripe, or while they're "green." Once ripened they are red or even darker. Only ripened chiles are dried and ground. Although chiles are often called "peppers," this term is misleading because while they are related to bell peppers, they contain oils that give them their characteristic heat.

Climate and soil conditions affect the heat of chiles, so it makes sense that the extra-dry soil and hot climate of New Mexico produce the hottest chiles. The heat of a chile comes from a substance called *capsaicin* found in its veins, and to a much lesser extent in its seeds. When handling fresh chiles you should wear rubber or plastic gloves. Be sure to avoid touching your eyes and to wash your hands thoroughly when you're done. I have yet to find a truly effective antidote to burns from a mean jalapeño!

The heat of chiles is relative, as far as the human palate is concerned; a jalapeño that seems fiery to one person might seem mild to another. Generally, the smaller the chile, the hotter it is. When I teach classes on chiles I like to use the analogy of the scorpions that inhabit the southwestern desert: They range in size from large to quite small, the smallest being the deadliest. The same goes for chiles—the smallest are the most searingly hot!

Fresh and Canned Chiles

Anaheim
Named after the California city, Anaheim chiles are also called California green chiles. The most common variety of large chile, Anaheims are slim and four to six inches long. Ranging from mild to hot, depending on growing conditions, roasted Anaheims are available canned (they are called mild green chiles), either chopped or whole. These chiles turn red when fully ripe; ripe Anaheims are dried and called *chile Colorado* or sometimes *New Mexico chiles*. Whole chiles Colorado are commonly made into decorative wreaths or strings (*ristras*). However, when chiles Colorado are ground they make one of the most frequently used spices in southwestern cooking: red chile powder (see Dried Chiles).

Jalapeño
Jalapeños are small, very hot chiles named for Jalapa, a city in Mexico. They are dark green, fat, and about three inches long. Fresh jalapeños will ripen to red. Jalapeños are available fresh, canned, and pickled (*en escabeche*). Smoked, dried jalapeños (*chipotle*) are sold either loose (a dull wrinkled brown) or canned in a highly spiced red sauce called adobo sauce. Jalapeños are readily available in grocery stores.

Mirasol
Mirasol means "looking at the sun," a reference to these peppers' yellow color. Mirasols are about two inches long and give food a yellow color, some heat, and a good flavor.

Poblano
Poblanos are dark green and three to four inches long with an elongated bell shape. They vary from mild to medium-hot and are used most often for *chiles rellenos* (stuffed chiles).

Serrano
Serrano chiles are small, flavorful, and very hot. Green, but ripening to a bright red, serranos are smaller, shorter, and even hotter than jalapeños. They are available fresh and canned.

Roasting and Peeling Fresh Chiles
Roasting (parching) fresh green chiles gives them a distinctive, smoky flavor. Flame-roasting, broiling, or grilling chiles blisters their waxy outer skin, which then can be peeled off. To flame-roast a chile, pierce it with a long-handled fork, and rotate it over the flame of a gas range until it is charred black and blistered (about 5 minutes). To broil chiles place them on a baking sheet 3 to 4 inches from the heat source. Broil the chiles, turning them frequently until they blister (12 to 17 minutes). After blistering chiles by either technique, place them in a plastic bag and close it tightly. Let the chiles stand until they are cool enough to handle (about 20 minutes). The chiles will steam in the bag, making peeling a breeze. You can remove the seeds if you so desire. Roasted chiles (peeled or unpeeled) freeze well.

Dried Chiles

Dried chiles are made from ripened (red) chiles. The ground red chile used for sauces and as the base for seasoning blends can be made from any of these dried chiles, often from a combination of mild and hot chiles.

Ancho The ripened, dried poblano chile is called an ancho. It's sweet and slightly hot.

Cascabel A round (about 1 inch in diameter), very hot chile, cascabels are less common than other dried chiles but have a delicious nutlike flavor when toasted. *Cascabel* means "rattle"; the seeds rattle when the chile is shaken.

Cayenne Very small and thin, these dried red chiles are burning hot. They are used in Asian and Cajun cooking as well as southwestern, and are available whole or ground.

Chile Colorado Dried ripe (red) Anaheim chiles are called chiles Colorado, or sometimes New Mexico chiles. They are the chile most often used to make red chile powder.

Chipotle The chipotle chile is a jalapeño that has been smoked and dried.

Pasilla (Chile Negro) These dried chiles are dark brownish-black, medium-sized, and very hot. They are often used in combination with anchos.

Red Pepper Flakes These flakes are made from dried red chiles, complete with seeds, and are usually very hot. Many Italian restaurants and pizza parlors serve these flakes in shakers. In southwestern cooking they are used to add heat and flavor, like any other chile.

Toasting and Grinding Dried Chiles

Toasting dried chiles before grinding them imparts a nice flavor and stiffens their outer skin, making the chiles easier to grind. Use care when toasting chiles because they burn easily. One method is to roast whole chiles in an ungreased skillet for a few minutes, shaking the pan constantly, until they are fragrant. Another method is to place chiles on a baking sheet and roast them in a 350° oven for a few minutes, watching them carefully and turning them once. Cool the toasted chiles, break them apart, and discard the stems, seeds, and inner veins. Grind the chiles to a fine powder in a blender or clean coffee grinder. Store the ground chile in an airtight container in a cool, dark place and use it to make sauces or season any dish.

Beginning Fajitas

You can make wonderful fajitas using almost any kind of meat. Here are some favorite choices, with hints on their preparation. Many meats are marinated before cooking to add flavor. Meat can be marinated whole or in strips or chunks. If you plan to cut up the meat for cooking, do so before marinating it. Feel free to experiment with marinades as you would with spices.

Selecting Meats, Poultry, Game, and Shrimp

Beef Lean, economical cuts of beef are perfect for marinating and grilling. To make these cuts tender, slice them across the grain after the marinating or cooking.

Skirt Steak or Fajita This is the beef cut traditionally used in Texas for the dish now known as fajitas. Skirt steak is a lean, somewhat tough piece of meat taken from the diaphragm. At one time it was an inexpensive cut that was often just ground up for hamburger—except in the Southwest. As fajitas have grown in popularity, skirt steak has become more expensive, but it is still a delicious choice for marinating and grilling. Trim all excess fat and membrane from the steak and cut it into smaller steaks to marinate (if desired) and cook. (A full skirt steak is quite large—4 to 5 inches wide, 2 to 3 feet long and up to 1 inch thick.) For quicker cooking, a 1-inch-thick steak can be butterflied and cut into smaller steaks.

Flank Steak Cut flank steak into smaller steaks for easier handling.

Rib-eye Steak Rib-eye steaks can be either cooked whole and then sliced, or cut into strips before cooking.

Chuck Steak Chuck steaks (1-inch-thick) are cut from a boneless shoulder.

Top Round Steak (London Broil) Steaks should be ½ to 1 inch thick. After cooking they should be cut diagonally across the grain to keep them tender.

Pork Boneless, center-cut pork loin roast or pork tenderloin is lean and can be cut in cubes, strips, or slices for marinating and cooking.

Lamb The leanest cuts are from boneless leg or shoulder; they can be cut into cubes or strips.

Poultry Poultry has long been used in southwestern cooking, and it suits those people who either do not eat red meat or just want lighter fare. Chicken and turkey are inexpensive and easily available, but you can also use game poultry.

Chicken Boneless, skinless breasts and thighs are good choices.

Turkey Boneless breast tenderloins or slices are excellent for fajitas. Turkey is a native American bird used frequently in the Southwest, especially smoked.

Game and Shrimp
Game meats are used throughout the Southwest; some game animals are even raised domestically. Not all kinds of game are appropriate for grilling, but the following work well. Shrimp, traditionally found in the Gulf of Mexico or on the west Mexican coast, are sometimes served in fajitas as well.

Venison Deer meat is lean and flavorful. Cut it either into strips for kabobs or into steaks to grill or broil quickly. A fruity marinade complements the richer flavor of venison well.

Duck Boneless duck breasts, quickly grilled or pan-fried and then sliced, give a new twist to fajitas.

Shrimp Use medium- to jumbo-sized shrimp for marinating and grilling. Shrimp can also be sautéed and served wrapped in tortillas, with salsas on the side.

Marinating Meats

Grilling meat over charcoal gives it a mouth-watering flavor and aroma, but marinating meat before grilling yields an even more complex, intense taste. Marinades serve a threefold purpose: tenderizing, moisturizing, and enhancing flavor.

A marinade is a seasoned liquid that usually contains an acidic ingredient (vinegar, wine, citrus or fruit juice, or yogurt) that penetrates meat fibers and helps tenderize them. Adding oil lubricates the meat, and adding herbs, spices, and seasonings (garlic, onion, citrus peel, chiles) provides flavor, aroma, and zest. The flavors chosen should complement the natural flavors of the meat.

A note about tenderizing: Marinades only tenderize meat down to ¼ inch from the cut surface, so thin pieces work best for tenderizing. The acid in the marinade breaks down the meat's protein structure, softening its texture. Don't marinate longer than 24 hours, or the meat will get mushy.

Marinating Tips
1. Place meat in a container that won't react to the acid in the marinade (glass, glazed ceramic, stainless steel, or a recloseable plastic bag).
2. The marinade should be cool when poured over the meat.
3. Immerse the meat in the marinade. Turn the meat occasionally during marinating to expose all sides to the seasoning.
4. Always marinate meat in the refrigerator; just remove it a few minutes before cooking to take the chill off.
5. Marinate meat at least 4 hours for maximum flavor. Shrimp need only 1 to 2 hours; marinating it longer can make it too soft.
6. Salt tends to draw the natural juices out of meats, so don't include it in marinades. Instead, season the meat with salt after it is cooked.
7. Use the marinade to baste the meat during grilling or broiling. If you want to serve the marinade as a sauce with the meat, heat it to boiling first to kill any bacteria from the raw meat.
8. Discard any marinade that is not used for basting or sauce.

Tex-Mex Marinade

Ingredients

½ cup lime juice

*⅓ cup **each** olive oil and tequila*

4 cloves garlic, crushed

1 tablespoon chopped fresh cilantro leaves

1½ teaspoons ground cumin

1 teaspoon dried oregano leaves, crushed

Directions

In small bowl, whisk all ingredients together.

Makes about 1⅓ cups

Cowboy Marinade

Ingredients

⅓ cup cider vinegar

3 tablespoons Worcestershire sauce

1 tablespoon brown sugar

1¾ teaspoons dry mustard

2 cloves garlic

1 cup vegetable oil

Directions

In blender, combine vinegar, Worcestershire sauce, sugar, mustard, and garlic. Blend until smooth; slowly pour oil in, with motor running, until emulsified.

Makes about 1⅔ cups

Brewer's Marinade

Ingredients

1 can (12 oz.) beer

1 medium onion, chopped

¼ cup Dijon-style mustard

2 tablespoons vegetable oil

8 to 10 peppercorns

1 tablespoon chopped celery leaves

*1 teaspoon **each** dried rosemary leaves (crushed) and ground cumin*

1 clove garlic, crushed

1 bay leaf, crumbled

Directions

In medium bowl, whisk all ingredients together. Great with pork, chicken, turkey, or venison.

Makes about 3¾ cups

Tropical Marinade

Ingredients

*1½ cups **each** pineapple juice and dry red wine*

¼ cup packed brown sugar

1½ tablespoons grated onion

*1½ teaspoons **each** Worcestershire sauce and dried thyme leaves, crushed*

¾ teaspoon dry mustard

¼ teaspoon freshly ground pepper

2 cloves garlic, crushed

Directions

In medium bowl, whisk all ingredients together.

Makes about 3¼ cups

Savory Marinade

Use this marinade for 1½ lbs. flank or skirt steak:

Ingredients

½ *cup olive oil*

¼ *cup **each** lime juice and red wine vinegar*

1 medium onion, chopped

1 clove garlic, crushed

1 teaspoon chili powder

¼ *teaspoon ground cumin*

Directions

In small bowl, whisk all ingredients together.

Makes about 2 cups

Cooking Techniques

Grilling The emphasis on grilling in southwestern cuisine comes from the nomadic lifestyle of the cowboys, ranchers, and Indians that inhabited the land. People on the move had few opportunities to use such permanent structures as ovens, so many southwestern dishes relied on simply grilling or broiling meat over a fire. Today we have many options for cooking meat, but if you can, try a little authenticity and use a grill.

Building a fire:
1. Open any vents in the bottom of the grill.
2. Use enough charcoal to cover an area 1 or 2 inches bigger than the area the food will cover on the grill.
3. Either pile the briquets in a mound or place them in a chimney starter, and ignite.

4. When the coals are ash-covered (30 to 45 minutes), spread them in a single layer and check their temperature (see How Hot Is the Fire? next page).
5. You can use aromatic wood chips to produce a more flavorful smoke. Mesquite (which is native to the Southwest), hickory, maple, and oak produce the most strongly scented smoke. Soak the chips in water for 30 minutes, then toss them on top of the hot coals. The moisture will make the coals smolder, sending more wood flavor up to the food. Placing moistened sprigs of fresh herbs (rosemary, thyme) on the coals smells good, but doesn't really affect the food. Instead, while the meat is marinating, infuse olive oil with chopped fresh herbs, citrus peels, red pepper flakes, chopped garlic, or ground cumin and use the flavored oil to baste the meat or vegetables. You can also try Tex-Mex Oil.

Tex-Mex Oil

Ingredients

6 tablespoons olive oil

½ teaspoon **each** ground cumin and oregano leaves

¼ teaspoon **each** dried red pepper flakes and crushed fennel seed

2 tablespoons chopped fresh cilantro leaves

2 cloves of garlic, crushed

Directions

Mix all ingredients together. Let stand at room temperature at least 4 hours.

How Hot Is the Fire?

To check the temperature of the fire, carefully hold the palm of your hand about 4 inches above the coals. Count the number of seconds before you must pull your hand away from the heat.

Time	Temperature
2 seconds	hot (high)
3 seconds	medium-hot
4 seconds	medium
5 seconds	low

Three to four seconds means you have the ideal temperature for open-grilling meats. Five seconds indicates a lower heat perfect for vegetables and fruits.

The Grill's Ready. . .

1. Grease the grill grid and place it 4 to 6 inches over the coals (depending on the food you are grilling).
2. Use long-handled tongs or a spatula to handle the meat; piercing it with a fork allows juices to escape.
3. Grill baskets should be greased and preheated on the grill before they are filled.
4. If you want to use a barbecue sauce with honey, sugar, or tomato, brush it onto the meat in the last 10 minutes of grilling, to prevent burning.
5. To see whether the meat is done, use a sharp knife to make a slit near the bone or the center of the piece.

Broiling

If time is short, it's snowing outside, or you're out of charcoal, broiling is the next best way to cook your fajitas. Beef steaks ¾ to 1 inch thick can be seared in a hot skillet over high heat for 2 minutes per side, then broiled for 5 minutes or until done. Broil any food on a rack in a broiler pan about 4 inches from the heat source.

Pan-Frying or Sautéing

Pan-frying is a good, quick technique for more thinly cut, tender pieces of meat such as tenderloin or rib-eye steaks. Sear the meat in some vegetable oil over high heat for about 30 seconds per side or until done. Strips of meat or poultry can be sautéed over medium-high heat in some olive oil or Tex-Mex Oil (page 21) until done.

Deep-Frying

Deep-frying strips of meat or poultry makes them very tender. In a large saucepan or deep-fryer, heat 3 cups of vegetable oil to 400°. (Peanut oil is more stable at high temperatures than other oils because it does not break down easily; it therefore has a higher smoke point.) Use tongs to immerse thin, 4- to 5-inch-long pieces of meat or poultry in the hot oil. Fry the meat for 40 to 50 seconds or until it is browned on both sides. Drain the cooked meat on paper towels.

Warming Tortillas

Warming tortillas not only makes them easier to wrap around food but also makes them more tender. Spread with herb butter, warm tortillas are as much a simple pleasure as fresh bread right out of the oven. Several methods can be used to warm tortillas for serving with fajitas:

1. Lay tortillas directly on hot grill, one at a time, just before eating. Brush with flavored olive oil, if desired.

2. Heat tortillas on hot ungreased griddle or skillet, or on a comal, if you have one.

3. Wrap 6 tortillas in aluminum foil. Bake in 300° oven 15 minutes, or until hot.

4. Wrap 6 tortillas in damp dish towel or plastic wrap. Microwave on high (100%) 1 minute.

The final trick is keeping the tortillas warm throughout a meal. You can buy terra cotta tortilla warmers that can be preheated in the oven and will hold the heat. But I've found the simplest solution: just keep the warm tortillas wrapped in foil and use them one at a time!

Building a Neater Fajita

(Or, How to Avoid the Laundry After Dinner...)

Well, avoiding the laundry might not be possible, since fajitas are an inherently messy food. But fajitas' messiness is also half their fun! Following a few simple assembly instructions, however, will help keep the mess to a minimum. Here are some tips for putting together an official fajita.

Have any or all of the following fixin's on hand:

A selection of salsas
Pico de Gallo (see page 56)
Sliced or chopped fresh jalapeño chiles
Fresh cilantro leaves
Lime wedges (for squeezing juice)
Dairy sour cream

Guacamole
Warm flour tortillas (6- to 7-inch)
Sizzling hot grilled, broiled, sautéed,
or deep-fried meat strips
Stewed beans
Rice

First, take a tortilla in hand and lay a few strips of meat across the center of it. Now begin to add some dips and dabs of whatever fixin's you want. Beware of letting your eyes get bigger than your tortilla, or you'll have a real mess when you fold up your fajita (and you'll definitely have to make a run for the laundry!). Remember, there are always more tortillas! Next, fold up one side of the tortilla at the long end of the meat strips, then fold the sides over, forming a sort of burrito with one end open. This technique should result in a fajita that will catch—at least for the first few bites—leaking salsa. Wash it all down with cold beer (preferably Mexican) or Margaritas, if desired. This method is only one of many—whip up some fixin's and devise your own!

Drinks, Appetizers, and Snacks

Many southwestern drinks (*botanas*) and appetizers (*antojitos*) have become well known and popular outside the Southwest (Margaritas, Nachos, Chiles Con Queso, chips and salsa). They are an important part of the colorful, abundant food considered so necessary at the southwestern table. Foods traditionally served as appetizers are often expanded to become main courses, while salads, vegetable relishes, or condiments (guacamole, salsas) become appetizers. I've developed an assortment of recipes that include traditional offerings (Antojitos Platter, Tucson Cheese Crisps, Layered Kidney Bean Dip) as well as some lighter, more unusual fare (Zippy Pepita and Pine Nut Mix, Nogales Popcorn Mix). Don't forget to mix up cool, refreshing *bebidas* to wash down the spicy food (Watermelon-Strawberry Refreshers, Piña Coladas, Blushing Sangria).

Watermelon-Strawberry Refreshers

Watermelons and strawberries from Mexico combine to make fancy fruit slushes.

Ingredients

4 cups 1-inch watermelon chunks, seeded

2 cups strawberries, hulled and halved

1¼ cups white rum or orange juice

6 tablespoons fresh lime juice

2 tablespoons sugar

Lime slices

Directions

1. Place watermelon chunks and strawberries in a large plastic bag. Seal and freeze bag at least 4 hours.

2. Pour rum or orange juice, lime juice, and sugar into a 2-quart pitcher; stir to dissolve sugar.

3. In blender or food processor, purée watermelon and strawberries, in batches, about 1 minute each.

4. Serve in stemmed glasses, garnished with lime slices.

Variations: Substitute 6 cups frozen chunks of pineapple, cantaloupe, and/or honeydew melon for watermelon and strawberries.

Makes 6 servings

Blushing Sangria

You'll enjoy this lighter version of the classic Sangria; it's made with white wine instead of red.

Ingredients

⅓ cup **each** sugar and orange-flavored liqueur

2 small oranges, thinly sliced

1 cup sliced strawberries

1 bottle (750 ml) **each** dry white wine and White Zinfandel wine, chilled

¼ cup sweetened lime juice

1 quart lemon-lime soda, chilled

Directions

1. In medium bowl, combine sugar and liqueur; stir to dissolve sugar.

2. Add orange and strawberry slices. Cover and marinate 2 hours.

3. In large punch bowl, combine wines, sweetened lime juice, soda, and undrained marinated fruit. Stir well.

Makes 12 servings

Frozen Margaritas

There's nothing better than one of these sweet-tart Margaritas to cut the heat of chiles!

Ingredients

⅔ cup **each** tequila and lime juice

⅓ cup **each** Triple Sec and water

¼ cup superfine sugar

Ice

Lime wedges

Coarse salt

Directions

1. In blender container that holds at least 5 cups of liquid, place tequila, lime juice, Triple Sec, water, and sugar.

2. Add enough ice to bring liquid level to 5 cups. Blend at highest speed until ice is finely crushed.

3. Rub edges of 6 chilled goblets or wine glasses with lime wedges. Dip rims in coarse salt.

4. Fill glasses with Margaritas. Garnish with lime slices, if desired.

Makes 6 servings

Piña Coladas

One sip and you'll be transported to a sunny beach in Mexico!

Ingredients

2 cups crushed ice

1 cup light rum*

*¾ cup **each** cream of coconut and chilled pineapple juice*

Fresh pineapple spears

Mint sprigs

Directions

1. In blender, combine all ingredients except pineapple spears and mint. Blend at high speed until frothy.

2. Pour into chilled tall or stemmed glasses. Garnish with pineapple spears and/or mint sprigs.

*For a nonalcoholic drink, substitute ½ cup half-and-half and ½ cup pineapple juice for rum.

Makes 4 servings

Sun Tea

Try freezing mint leaves in ice cubes or making ice cubes from pineapple, tangerine, or orange juice for a fun and flavorful addition to Sun Tea.

Ingredients

3 bags regular, decaffeinated, or herbal tea

8 cups water

Mint Syrup (see below)

Directions

1. Place tea bags in ½-gallon bottle or jar; pour water over bags.

2. Place bottle or jar in hot sun and let stand at least 3 hours.

3. Serve over ice and sweeten with Mint Syrup, if desired.

Makes ½ gallon

Mint Syrup

Ingredients

1⅔ cups sugar

1 cup water

¼ cup chopped fresh mint

Directions

1. In medium saucepan, combine all ingredients.

2. Bring mixture to a boil, stirring and washing down any sugar crystals on sides of pan with a brush dipped in cold water, until sugar is dissolved.

3. Cook syrup over medium heat 5 minutes without stirring.

4. Cool syrup and strain into small jar or bottle. Discard mint.

5. Seal and refrigerate up to 1 month.

Makes about 1 cup

Spicy Rosemary Lemonade

The subtle flavor of rosemary with lemon and some hot chile makes a surprisingly thirst-quenching drink.

Ingredients

1 cup water

1 cup sugar

*2 teaspoons fresh rosemary leaves (or
1 teaspoon dried rosemary leaves)*

½ teaspoon dried crushed red chile

3 cups water

⅔ cup lemon juice

Thin lemon slices

Directions

1. In small saucepan, bring water, sugar, rosemary, and crushed chile to a boil; boil 5 minutes. Strain mixture and cool.

2. In large pitcher, pour 3 cups water and lemon juice. Add cooled syrup and stir well.

3. Serve over ice and garnish with lemon slices.

Makes 6 servings

Tortilla Chips

These chips are addicting, whether served with a spicy salsa, with bean dip, or alone!

Ingredients

12 yellow or blue corn (6-inch) or flour (8-inch) tortillas

Salt

Garlic salt

Cumin Salt (see below)

Melted butter or margarine

Vegetable oil (for deep-frying)

Directions

Baked Chips

1. Heat oven to 375°. Cut each tortilla into 8 wedges. If desired, use a 3-inch biscuit cutter to cut round chips. (Yield will be lower.)

2. In a 15×10×1-inch baking pan, place single layer of tortilla wedges. If desired, brush chips with melted butter or spritz with water. Sprinkle with salt, garlic salt, or Cumin Salt.

3. Bake until chips are golden brown, 7 to 10 minutes. Store airtight up to 2 weeks.

Deep-fried Chips

1. In large saucepan, heat 1 inch vegetable oil to 360°. Cut tortillas into wedges or circles, as in previous method.

2. Fry chips until golden brown, about 1 minute. Drain on paper towels. Sprinkle with salt, garlic salt, or Cumin Salt. Store airtight up to 2 weeks.

Makes 8 dozen

Cumin Salt

Ingredients

1 teaspoon coarse salt

½ teaspoon **each** ground cumin and celery salt

¼ teaspoon **each** cayenne pepper and garlic powder

Directions

In a small bowl, mix all ingredients together.

Antojitos Platter

An appetizing tray of crunchy vegetables with a touch of sweet fruit is a welcome start to any southwestern meal.

Ingredients

1 small (about 3 lbs.) pineapple

1 lb. jicama

2 medium cucumbers

1 bunch radishes, stemmed and cleaned

⅓ cup lime juice

¼ cup salt

1 tablespoon paprika

1 teaspoon chili powder

Lime wedges

Directions

1. Cut unpeeled pineapple crosswise into ½-inch slices; remove core and cut each slice into quarters.

2. Peel jicama. Cut into ½ × ½ × 2-inch sticks.

3. Cut each cucumber lengthwise into quarters, then cut each quarter into 2-inch pieces.

4. Coat pineapple, jicama, cucumbers, and radishes with lime juice. Arrange on serving platter.

5. In small serving bowl, mix salt, paprika, and chili powder. Place in center of serving platter with lime wedges.

6. To eat, squeeze lime wedges over pineapple and vegetables and dip in seasoned salt.

Makes 8 servings

Classic Nachos

You can substitute Co-Jack cheese for the Cheddar and Monterey Jack when making this traditional appetizer.

Ingredients

36 unsalted corn tortilla chips

5 pickled jalapeño chiles, sliced

1½ cups diced tomatoes

1 can (2.25 oz.) sliced ripe olives, drained

1½ cups shredded sharp Cheddar cheese

1 cup shredded Monterey Jack cheese

4 green onions, sliced (including green)

Guacamole

Dairy sour cream

Salsa

Directions

1. Heat oven to 475°. In 15×10×1-inch jelly-roll pan arrange chips. Sprinkle with chiles, tomatoes, and olives. Sprinkle cheeses on top.

2. Bake until cheese is melted and bubbly, about 5 minutes. Sprinkle with green onions and serve with dollops of guacamole, sour cream, and salsa.

Makes 4 to 6 servings

Tucson Cheese Crisps

I grew up in Tucson, Arizona, snacking on cheese crisps everyday after school. Feel free to use other cheeses, but Cheddar is traditional.

Ingredients

2 (12- or 10-inch) flour tortillas*

2 tablespoons butter or margarine, softened

2 cups shredded Longhorn Cheddar cheese

2 green onions, thinly sliced (including green)

Tomato salsa

Guacamole

Directions

1. Heat oven to 400°. Spread tortillas with butter and place on baking sheet. Bake until lightly browned and crisp, 2 to 3 minutes.

2. Sprinkle tortillas with cheese. Place under broiler until cheese is melted and bubbly.

3. Sprinkle with onions and serve immediately. Serve with salsa and guacamole. Each person breaks off a piece of crisp and adds condiments to taste.

Makes 4 servings

*In Arizona restaurants, 18-inch tortillas are commonly used for crisps that are served on large pizza pans. The pan is set on a stand over a lighted candle that keeps the crisp warm.

Layered Kidney Bean Dip

Mashed kidney beans with bacon or spicy chorizo replace refried pinto beans in this version of a popular appetizer bean dip.

Ingredients

6 slices bacon, chopped, or 1 cup crumbled chorizo sausage

½ cup chopped onion

½ teaspoon chili powder

1 can (16 oz.) kidney beans, drained (reserve ¼ cup liquid)

2 cups guacamole

1 cup dairy sour cream

1 cup shredded Co-Jack cheese

¼ cup sliced green onion (including green)

Cilantro leaves

Sliced ripe olives

Tortilla chips

Fresh vegetable sticks (jicama, carrot, zucchini)

Directions

1. In medium skillet, sauté bacon or chorizo, onion, and chili powder over medium heat until bacon is crisp, 8 to 10 minutes, or until chorizo is browned. Drain well and cool.

2. In large bowl, coarsely mash beans; stir in reserved bean liquid and bacon or chorizo mixture.

3. Spread bean mixture into 8-inch circle on a large platter. Spread guacamole, then sour cream, evenly on top.

4. Sprinkle sour cream with cheese, then green onions. Garnish with cilantro and olives.

5. Serve with chips and vegetables.

Makes 6 to 8 servings

Chiles con Queso

This cheese sauce with green chiles is easy to keep warm in a crockpot for parties—don't forget the homemade tortilla chips!

Ingredients

2 tablespoons vegetable oil

1 medium onion, chopped

2 cloves garlic, finely chopped

1 serrano chile, seeded and finely chopped

½ cup diced tomatoes

1 can (4 oz.) chopped green chiles, undrained

½ cup whipping cream

2 cups shredded Longhorn Cheddar, Chihuahua, or Asadero cheese (or a combination)

Tortilla chips

Directions

1. In 1-quart saucepan or heatproof dish, heat oil over medium heat until hot. Sauté onion, garlic, and serrano chile until tender, about 7 minutes. Stir in tomatoes.

2. Add green chiles and cream. Cook, stirring, until hot. Reduce heat to low and stir in cheese until melted.

3. Keep cheese dip warm in chafing dish, fondue pot, or small crock pot, or on electric warming tray. Serve with tortilla chips.

Makes about 3 cups

Nogales Popcorn Mix

The Southwest Seasoning Mix (below) can be used to season ground meat for tacos, to spice chili, or to add a southwestern flavor to any food you choose.

Ingredients

4 cups popped corn

2 cups broken yellow or blue corn tortilla chips

3 tablespoons butter or margarine, melted

1½ tablespoons Southwest Seasoning Mix (see below) or commercial taco seasoning mix

Directions

1. In large bowl, combine popcorn and chips.

2. In small bowl, mix butter and seasoning mix. Pour over popcorn mix and toss well.

Makes 6 cups

Southwest Seasoning Mix

Ingredients

3 tablespoons ground red chile (mild, medium, or hot)

*2 tablespoons **each** paprika and yellow corn meal*

*1 tablespoon **each** ground coriander and dried parsley, crushed*

2 teaspoons ground cumin

*1 teaspoon **each** salt and dried oregano leaves, crushed*

*¼ teaspoon **each** cayenne pepper and garlic powder*

Directions

In small bowl, mix all ingredients well. Store in airtight container.

Makes about ⅔ cup

Zippy Pepita and Pine Nut Mix

Look for fresh pumpkin seeds (pepitas) and pine nuts at your local co-op or health food store.

Ingredients

*1½ cups **each** hulled raw pumpkin seeds and pine nuts*

1 tablespoon olive oil

2 tablespoons medium-hot ground red chile

1 tablespoon ground cumin

1½ teaspoons salt

½ teaspoon freshly ground pepper

Directions

1. In large skillet, toast pumpkin seeds and pine nuts over medium heat until fragrant, about 4 to 5 minutes.

2. Stir in remaining ingredients until well coated. Cool.

3. Refrigerate in airtight container up to 3 months.

Makes 3 cups

Green Chile Dip

Try roasting and peeling fresh green Anaheim chiles instead of using canned for an even fresher flavor.

Ingredients

1 cup dairy sour cream

⅓ cup lightly packed parsley

2 green onions, cut into 1-inch pieces (including green)

¾ teaspoon garlic salt

¼ teaspoon dried oregano leaves

1 can (4 oz.) chopped green chiles, drained

Tortilla chips

Fresh vegetable sticks (jicama, carrot, zucchini)

Directions

1. In food processor, combine sour cream, parsley, onions, garlic salt, and oregano. Process until smooth.

2. Pour mixture into serving bowl; stir in chiles. Serve with tortilla chips and/or vegetable dippers.

Makes about 1¾ cups

Sweet Potato and Plantain Chips

A nice change from potato chips!

Ingredients

3 medium sweet potatoes, peeled and cut into
1/16-inch slices

3 medium plantains, peeled and cut into
1/4-inch slices

Vegetable oil

1 tablespoon chili powder

Salt

Ice water

Directions

1. In large bowl, cover potato slices with ice water. Soak 30 minutes.

2. Meanwhile, in Dutch oven, heat 2 to 3 inches oil to 360°.

3. Fry plantain slices until golden brown, about 2 minutes. Drain on paper towels. Toss with chili powder and salt to taste.

4. Drain potato slices and pat dry. Fry slices until light brown around edges, 1 to 2 minutes. Drain on paper towels. Toss with salt to taste.

5. Serve chips at room temperature. Store airtight up to a month.

Makes 4 to 6 servings

Soups and Salads

Traditionally, soups and stews in the Southwest were long-simmering, hearty affairs meant to be served as main courses. In recent years, however, a variety of lighter soups have joined the classic bean soups, stews, and chilis that remain part of southwest cooking today. These lighter combinations of vegetables or fruits now set the stage for the rest of the meal. Chilled soups have also become quite popular and are perfect to begin a meal of fajitas (Chilled Avocado Lemon Soup, Citrus Tomato Gazpacho). Cool, crisp salads, made from the array of regional produce now available from Mexico and irrigated desert farmland, help to cut the heat of chiles (Jicama Julienne Salad, Cilantro and Red Pepper Slaw, Crispy Cucumber Salad).

Citrus Tomato Gazpacho

A touch of citrus gives this gazpacho a smooth, subtle flavor.

Ingredients

2 large ripe tomatoes, cut into quarters

2 medium green, red, or yellow bell peppers, cut into quarters

1 medium cucumber, cut into 1-inch pieces

4 green onions, cut into 1-inch pieces (including green)

2 cloves garlic, halved

2 cups tomato juice

1 cup fresh orange juice

¼ cup fresh cilantro leaves

3 tablespoons fresh lime juice

2 tablespoons olive oil

1½ teaspoons grated orange peel

½ teaspoon grated lime peel

Salt

Hot pepper sauce

Mexican Cream (see below)

Diced avocado

Directions

1. In food processor or blender,* coarsely chop tomatoes, peppers, cucumber, onion, and garlic. Remove half of mixture to large bowl.

2. Add tomato juice, orange juice, cilantro, lime juice, olive oil, and citrus peels to processor or blender. Process until nearly smooth. Pour mixture into bowl with other vegetables.

3. Mix soup well; season to taste with salt and hot pepper sauce. Serve topped with Mexican Cream and avocado.

*If using blender, process in batches.

Makes 6 to 8 servings

Mexican Cream

Ingredients

1 cup dairy sour cream

½ cup whipping cream

1 teaspoon fresh lime juice

Directions

1. In small bowl, blend all ingredients.

2. Cover and let stand at room temperature 2 hours to thicken. Refrigerate.

Makes about 1½ cups

White Gazpacho

I first tried this wonderful, white, garlicky version of gazpacho at a deli that serves ethnic "street food." It's a delicious alternative to tomato-based gazpacho.

Ingredients

¼ cup packed parsley leaves

3 cloves garlic

1 teaspoon dried basil leaves

½ teaspoon dried oregano leaves

1 medium (about 1 lb.) European seedless cucumber, cut up

1 medium green pepper, seeded and quartered

1 small white onion, quartered

3 green onions, cut into 1-inch pieces (including green)

2 cups low-fat plain yogurt

3 cups chicken broth

2 tablespoons lemon juice

Hot pepper sauce

Salt

Chopped tomatoes

Sliced ripe olives

Toasted almond slivers

Directions

1. In food processor or blender, finely chop parsley, garlic, basil, and oregano. Add cucumber, green pepper, and onions; process until coarsely chopped.

2. Blend in yogurt, broth, and lemon juice until well mixed. Season to taste with hot pepper sauce and salt.

3. Cover and refrigerate until chilled. Serve garnished with tomatoes, olives, and/or almonds.

Makes 6 servings

Chilled Avocado Lemon Soup

The tartness of both lemon and buttermilk balances the richness of avocado to create a unique flavor. Instead of pumpkin seeds for garnish, try crumbled fried bacon.

Ingredients

1 tablespoon vegetable oil

½ cup chopped onion

3 large ripe avocados, pitted and peeled

½ cup lemon juice

2½ cups chicken broth

½ teaspoon hot pepper sauce (or to taste)

1½ cups buttermilk

Salt

Salted pumpkin seeds

Mexican Cream (see page 44)

Directions

1. In small skillet, heat oil over medium heat. Sauté onion until tender, about 6 minutes. Set aside.

2. Slice avocados into blender. Add sautéed onion and lemon juice. Blend until smooth.

3. Add broth and hot pepper sauce to blender and blend until well mixed.

4. Pour avocado mixture into large bowl; stir in buttermilk. Season to taste with salt.

5. Cover and refrigerate at least 4 hours or overnight. Serve with pumpkin seeds and Mexican Cream.

Makes 6 servings

Calico Vegetable Chili

Serve this hearty meatless chili either as a light entrée or to begin a savory meal of fajitas.

Ingredients

2 tablespoons olive oil

2 cups chopped onion

4 cloves garlic, finely chopped

2 medium carrots, diced into ½-inch pieces

2 ribs celery, diced into ½-inch pieces

2 tablespoons chili powder

2 teaspoons dried rosemary, crushed

½ teaspoon cayenne pepper

1 **each** medium yellow summer squash, zucchini, green bell pepper, red bell pepper, diced into ½-inch pieces

1 jalapeño, seeded and finely chopped

2 medium tomatoes, seeded and chopped

1 can (16 oz.) tomato sauce with herbs

3 cups chicken broth

2 cans (16 oz. **each**) kidney beans, rinsed and drained

2 tablespoons masa flour

Shredded sharp Cheddar cheese

Dairy sour cream

Plain low-fat yogurt

Directions

1. In Dutch oven, heat oil over medium-high heat. Sauté onion and garlic 5 minutes. Add carrots and celery; sauté 4 minutes longer.

2. Reduce heat to low. Add chili powder, rosemary, and cayenne. Stir and cook until carrots are nearly tender. Add squash, zucchini, green and red peppers, and jalapeño; cook 5 minutes.

3. Stir in tomatoes, tomato sauce, and broth. Simmer uncovered until vegetables are tender, about 30 minutes. Stir in beans.

4. In small bowl, mix masa with enough cold water to make a watery paste. Slowly stir into chili. Bring to a boil and stir until thickened.

5. Serve hot with cheese or a dollop of sour cream or yogurt.

Makes 8 servings

Sopa de Maíz (Corn Soup)

Use Red Pepper Sauce and Parmesan Tortilla Strips (see below) to top salads as well as soups.

Ingredients

¼ cup butter or margarine

1 clove garlic, finely chopped

3½ cups fresh or frozen whole corn kernels

1 cup chicken broth

2 cups milk

1 teaspoon ground cumin

½ teaspoon dried oregano leaves, crushed

1 can (4 oz.) chopped green chiles

3 to 4 drops hot pepper sauce

Salt

Red Pepper Sauce (see below)

Parmesan Tortilla Strips (see below)

Directions

1. In 4-quart saucepan, melt butter over medium heat. Sauté garlic and corn 2 minutes. Remove from heat.

2. In blender, purée corn mixture with broth; return mixture to saucepan.

3. Stir in milk, cumin, oregano, green chiles, and hot pepper sauce. Bring mixture to boil over medium heat, stirring constantly. Remove from heat and season to taste with salt.

4. Serve bowls of soup with drizzle of Red Pepper Sauce and topped with Parmesan Tortilla Strips.

Makes 6 servings

Red Pepper Sauce

Ingredients

1 jar (7 oz.) chopped pimiento

2 tablespoons olive oil

2 cloves garlic

1 teaspoon lemon juice

½ teaspoon **each** dried oregano leaves and salt

2 drops hot pepper sauce

Directions

In blender, purée all ingredients together.

Parmesan Tortilla Strips

Ingredients

Vegetable oil

6 (6-inch) corn tortillas, cut in half, then cut crosswise into ¼-inch strips

6 tablespoons finely grated fresh Parmesan cheese

Directions

1. In large skillet, heat ½ inch oil. Fry tortilla strips in batches until golden and crisp. Remove from oil with slotted spoon; drain on paper towels.

2. Heat oven to 250°. In shallow baking pan, toss tortillas with cheese. Bake until cheese melts, about 5 minutes. Cool and store in airtight container. Will keep up to 1 week.

Iced Cantaloupe Soup

Sweet melons of all types are grown in Mexico and Arizona. This refreshing soup made from ripe cantaloupe is as pretty as it is delectable!

Ingredients

3 very ripe cantaloupe, halved and seeded

*6 tablespoons **each** orange-flavored liqueur (or orange juice) and heavy cream*

*3 tablespoons **each** sugar and lime juice*

*¼ teaspoon **each** ground cardamom and ground nutmeg*

Mint leaves

6 cantaloupe halves (optional)

Directions

1. In food processor or blender, process cantaloupe until smooth.

2. Add remaining ingredients and process until well blended. Refrigerate soup for 2 hours. Serve garnished with mint leaves in cantaloupe "bowl," if desired.

Makes 6 servings

Cilantro and Red Pepper Slaw

This crunchy coleslaw provides a refreshing contrast to a meal of fajitas or grilled foods.

Ingredients

1 small head cabbage, shredded

1 red bell pepper, cut in 1-inch julienne strips

½ small red onion, thinly sliced

½ cup chopped fresh cilantro leaves

½ cup vegetable oil

⅓ cup lime juice

2 cloves garlic, finely chopped

Salt

Freshly ground pepper

Directions

1. In large bowl, combine cabbage, red bell pepper, onion, and cilantro.

2. In small bowl, whisk together oil, lime juice, and garlic. Pour over salad mixture, tossing well. Season to taste with salt and pepper.

3. Cover and refrigerate at least 2 hours to allow flavors to blend.

Makes 6 to 8 servings

Marinated Melon Ball Salad

Freshly cracked black pepper has a sweetness that complements fresh fruit, especially melon.

Ingredients

2 cups **each** cantaloupe, honeydew melon, and watermelon balls

¾ cup orange juice

¼ cup lime juice

2 tablespoons honey

1 tablespoon chopped fresh mint

¼ cup orange-flavored liqueur (optional)

Freshly cracked black pepper (optional)

Directions

1. In large bowl, mix melon balls. Refrigerate.

2. In small saucepan, heat orange and lime juices, honey, and mint to boiling, stirring constantly. Remove from heat; stir in liqueur, if desired. Cool.

3. Pour cooled dressing over melon balls. Cover and refrigerate at least 2 hours. Serve with pepper, if desired.

Makes 6 servings

Crisp Cucumber Salad

Cucumbers have a cooling effect on hot chiles or spicy foods.

Ingredients

¾ cup **each** sugar, white distilled vinegar, and water

¾ teaspoon salt

½ teaspoon crushed red pepper flakes

2 large European cucumbers, thinly sliced

2 small red onions, thinly sliced

Fresh cilantro leaves

Directions

1. In small bowl, combine sugar, vinegar, water, salt, and red pepper flakes. Set aside.

2. In shallow 3-quart dish, place cucumbers and onions. Add vinegar mixture and toss gently. Cover and refrigerate at least 3 hours or overnight, stirring occasionally.

3. Drain and discard liquid. Place cucumbers and onions in serving bowl and garnish with cilantro.

Makes 6 servings

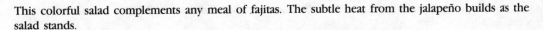

Black Bean Corn Salad

This colorful salad complements any meal of fajitas. The subtle heat from the jalapeño builds as the salad stands.

Ingredients

1 can (16 oz.) black beans, rinsed and drained

2 cups cooked fresh or frozen whole kernel corn

2 Italian plum (Roma) tomatoes or 1 medium red bell pepper, diced

4 green onions, sliced (including green)

1 jalapeño chile, seeded and finely chopped

2 tablespoons red wine vinegar or sherry vinegar

2 teaspoons cumin seeds, toasted and ground

1 teaspoon Dijon-style mustard

3 tablespoons olive oil

2 teaspoons chopped fresh cilantro leaves

Salt

Freshly ground pepper

Directions

1. In medium bowl, combine beans, corn, tomatoes or red bell pepper, onions, and jalapeño.

2. In small bowl, mix vinegar, cumin, and mustard. Slowly whisk in oil until well blended.

3. Pour dressing over bean mixture; stir in cilantro and season to taste with salt and pepper.

4. Cover and refrigerate 1 hour. To serve, bring to room temperature.

Makes 6 servings

Cilantro Pesto Potato Salad

Tender new potatoes and green beans in light cilantro yogurt sauce are a different way to serve potato salad.

Ingredients

2 lbs. red new potatoes, cooked and cooled

½ lb. green beans, cut into 1-inch pieces

½ cup **each** lightly packed parsley and fresh cilantro leaves

¼ cup grated Parmesan cheese

¾ cup low-fat plain yogurt

2 tablespoons orange juice

1 teaspoon grated orange peel

1 clove garlic

Salt

Freshly ground pepper

½ cup pecan halves, toasted and coarsely chopped

Directions

1. Cut potatoes into ¾-inch pieces. Place in large bowl.

2. Steam beans until tender, 5 to 10 minutes. Rinse with cold water, drain, and add to potatoes.

3. In blender or food processor, combine parsley, cilantro, cheese, yogurt, orange juice, orange peel, and garlic. Process until smooth.

4. Pour dressing over potato mixture and mix gently. Season to taste with salt and pepper. Cover and refrigerate up to 4 hours. Serve garnished with pecans.

Makes 6 servings

Jicama Julienne Salad

When I was a kid, my friends and I enjoyed pomegranate fights, using ripe fruit that had fallen from the trees. Our moms were less than happy, though, since pomegranate juice stains clothes a pretty pink!

Ingredients

1 lb. jicama, peeled and cut into 1½-inch matchsticks

Cumin Vinaigrette (see below)

2 red grapefruit or 3 oranges

1 large ripe avocado

2 green onions, sliced (including green)

Pomegranate seeds (optional)

Directions

1. In medium bowl, mix jicama with Cumin Vinaigrette. Cover and let stand 30 minutes.

2. With sharp paring knife, peel skin and white membrane from grapefruit or oranges. Cutting between membranes, remove fruit segments. Peel, pit, and slice avocado.

3. On each of four individual salad plates, mound one-fourth of jicama mixture. Surround each mound with slices of citrus and avocado.

4. Sprinkle each salad with green onion and pomegranate seeds, if desired.

Makes 4 servings

Cumin Vinaigrette

Ingredients

¼ cup olive oil

2 tablespoons red wine vinegar

1 tablespoon orange juice

1 teaspoon sugar

½ teaspoon ground cumin

1 clove garlic, crushed

Salt

Cayenne pepper

Directions

1. In small bowl, whisk together oil, vinegar, orange juice, sugar, cumin, and garlic.

2. Season to taste with salt and cayenne pepper.

Salsas and Condiments

No southwestern table is complete without at least one bowl of salsa or *picante* (hot) sauce. The Mexican tradition of seasoning food at the table has made spicy, flavorful salsas, relishes, and sauces an integral part of the southwestern meal. Used like salt and pepper in other parts of the country, salsas are combinations of dozens of different vegetables, fruits, chiles, herbs, and spices. Relishes and salsas (Jicama Papaya Relish, Salsa con Tequila) are generally chunky mixtures, while sauces (Chile Colorado, Salsa Verde) are smoother and usually spicier. Mix and match condiments to create new flavors with any meat, seafood, poultry, or tortilla dish. Other condiments (Honey Jalapeño Mustard, Rosy Salsa Mayonnaise, Herb Butters) are nontraditional, but use indigenous ingredients to give a southwestern twist to any food.

Pico de Gallo

Pico de Gallo, or "rooster's beak," also refers to a salad of orange and jicama. This salsa is a traditional condiment with fajitas.

Ingredients

1 large tomato, diced into ¾-inch pieces

1 small red onion, chopped

2 jalapeño chiles, finely chopped (including some seeds)

3 tablespoons chopped fresh cilantro leaves

Salt to taste

Directions

In small bowl, mix all ingredients.

Makes about 2 cups

Salsa Roja

Chipotle chiles are smoked jalapeños in a spiced sauce and are quite hot. Add more or less according to your preference.

Ingredients

1 small onion, cut up

2 ripe medium tomatoes, seeded and quartered

1 can (28 oz.) Italian plum (Roma) tomatoes, seeded and drained

2 cloves garlic, halved

2 canned chipotle chiles in adobo sauce, stemmed and seeded

1 tablespoon distilled white vinegar

1 teaspoon dried oregano

Directions

1. In food processor (or by hand), finely chop onion.

2. Add remaining ingredients and process with on/off bursts until well mixed yet still chunky.

3. Cover and refrigerate 1 hour to allow flavors to blend.

Makes 1 quart

Salsa Fresca

Fresh salsa should be eaten within a few days.

Ingredients

3 large ripe tomatoes, chopped

1 small white onion, chopped

2 to 3 fresh hot chiles (jalapeño or serrano), seeded and finely chopped

½ cup chopped fresh cilantro leaves

3 tablespoons lime juice or balsamic vinegar

Salt to taste

Directions

1. In medium bowl, mix all ingredients.

2. Cover and refrigerate at least 1 hour to allow flavors to blend.

Makes 3½ cups

Cherry Tomato Salsa

This salsa is particularly good as a chip dip.

Ingredients

2 pints cherry tomatoes, chopped

4 green onions, chopped (including green)

1 can (4 oz.) diced green chiles, undrained

1 can (4.25 oz.) chopped ripe olives, drained

3 tablespoons olive oil

2 tablespoons red wine vinegar

1 teaspoon garlic salt (or to taste)

Directions

1. In large bowl, mix all ingredients.

2. Cover and refrigerate at least 2 hours to allow flavors to blend.

Makes about 3 cups

Salsa con Tequila

Here's an unusual salsa made with a shot of tequila for a real Tex-Mex touch!

Ingredients

1 can (28 oz.) whole tomatoes, seeded, drained, and chopped

6 fresh mild green Anaheim chiles, roasted, peeled, and chopped, or 1 can (7 oz.) diced green chiles, undrained

½ cup chopped onion

2 canned pickled jalapeño chiles, chopped

1 clove garlic, finely chopped

2 tablespoons chopped fresh cilantro leaves

2½ tablespoons tequila

1 tablespoon olive oil

Salt to taste

Directions

1. In medium bowl, mix all ingredients.

2. Cover and refrigerate at least 2 hours to allow flavors to blend.

Makes about 2½ cups

Sage Salsa Fria

This salsa is especially good served with poultry.

Ingredients

3 ripe medium tomatoes, chopped

2 serrano chiles, seeded and finely chopped

1 small white onion, chopped

1 tablespoon chopped fresh sage or 1½ teaspoons dried sage, crushed

2 teaspoons rice vinegar or distilled white vinegar

1 teaspoon olive oil

Salt to taste

Directions

1. In medium bowl, mix all ingredients.

2. Cover and refrigerate at least 1 hour to allow flavors to blend.

Makes 3 cups

Chile Colorado (Red Chile Sauce)

Commonly known as enchilada sauce, Chile Colorado can be used to prepare chimichangas or enchiladas, to season beans, or to simmer meat. The heat level can be adjusted by using different types of ground red chile.

Ingredients

2 tablespoons olive oil, vegetable oil, or bacon fat

¼ cup finely chopped onion

1 clove garlic, crushed

1 teaspoon ground cumin

½ teaspoon dried oregano leaves, crushed

2 tablespoons all-purpose flour

½ cup ground red chile (mild, medium, or hot)

2 cups water

¾ teaspoon salt (or to taste)

Directions

1. In large skillet, heat oil over medium-high heat. Sauté onion and garlic until tender, about 4 minutes. Stir in cumin, oregano, and flour. Stir constantly and cook until mixture is bubbly and begins to brown, 2 to 3 minutes.

2. Reduce heat to medium and stir in ground chile. Blend in water and cook until sauce nearly boils, stirring constantly. (Watch carefully: chile burns easily!) Reduce heat to low and simmer 2 minutes, or until smooth and of desired consistency.

3. Season with salt. If a smoother sauce is desired, purée in blender or food processor.

Makes 2 cups

Sonoran Guacamole

This rich blend of avocado and tomato is perfect with fajitas or as a dip.

Ingredients

2 very ripe medium avocados, pitted and peeled

1 large tomato, seeded and diced

⅓ cup chopped onion

2 tablespoons canned diced green chiles

1 tablespoon lime juice

Hot pepper sauce to taste

Salt to taste

Directions

1. In medium bowl, mash avocado with fork.

2. Stir in remaining ingredients. Cover and refrigerate.

Makes 3 cups

The Scoop on Guacamole

There are as many variations of guacamole (avocado dip) as there are salsas, but the most classic blend is the simplest. For authentic guacamole the texture should be lumpy, so mash very ripe avocados roughly with a fork; food processors or blenders will not give the same texture. (In Mexico guacamole is made in a *molcajete* and *tejolote*, a three-legged mortar and pestle made from volcanic rock.) The addition of some hot chile, onion, tomato, lemon or lime juice, garlic, or cilantro depends on personal preference. I personally draw the line at mayonnaise, sour cream, or cream cheese; they mask the delicate, incomparable flavor and silkiness of perfectly ripe avocados.

Try not to make "guac" too far in advance; it's best freshly made, served at room temperature. However, it will keep well refrigerated up to three days; just be sure to press plastic wrap against the surface to prevent browning. Serve as an appetizer, salad, or condiment with any southwestern meal.

Chunky Guacamole

This "chunky" version is similar to an avocado salsa or salad.

Ingredients

2 large ripe avocados, pitted, peeled, and diced into ½-inch pieces

½ cup diced red or yellow bell pepper

2 green onions, sliced (including green)

1 jalapeño or serrano chile, seeded and finely chopped

1 clove garlic, finely chopped

1 tablespoon chopped fresh cilantro leaves

2 tablespoons lime juice

Salt to taste

Directions

1. In medium bowl, toss avocados, bell pepper, onions, chile, and garlic.

2. Stir in cilantro, lime juice, and salt. Cover and refrigerate.

Makes 3 cups

Tomatillo Salsa

An attractive pale green with a refreshing tartness, this green salsa is a nice alternative or supplement to tomato salsas.

Ingredients

½ lb. tomatillos, husks removed

⅓ cup coarsely chopped onion

2 jalapeño chiles, seeded and sliced

1 clove garlic, halved

¼ cup fresh cilantro leaves

2 tablespoons lemon juice

Salt

Directions

1. Cut tomatillos in quarters.

2. In food processor or blender, place tomatillos and remaining ingredients (except salt). Process until puréed. Season to taste with salt.

Makes 1⅔ cups

Salsa Verde

This thick green chile sauce is wonderful with enchiladas or tacos.

Ingredients

2 tablespoons vegetable oil

¼ cup chopped onion

1 clove garlic, finely chopped

2 tablespoons all-purpose flour

½ teaspoon ground cumin

1½ cups chicken broth

1 can (7 oz.) diced green chiles, undrained

1 tablespoon chopped canned jalapeño chile (or to taste)

1 tablespoon chopped fresh cilantro

Salt

Directions

1. In large skillet, heat oil over medium-high heat. Sauté onion and garlic until tender.

2. Stir in flour and cumin. Cook 2 to 3 minutes or until bubbly and beginning to brown.

3. Reduce heat to medium and slowly pour in chicken broth, stirring constantly.

4. Stir in remaining ingredients (except salt), bring mixture nearly to boil, reduce heat, and simmer 20 to 25 minutes or until thick. Season to taste with salt.

5. If desired, purée sauce in blender or food processor. Cover and refrigerate sauce up to 1 week. Reheat to use.

Makes 2 cups

Papaya Jicama Relish

This delicious salsa is best with rich meats, such as pork or lamb, or any grilled meat marinated in a sweet marinade.

Ingredients

2 ripe medium papayas, seeded and diced into ¼-inch pieces

¾ lb. jicama, peeled and diced into ¼-inch pieces (about 1 cup)

½ cup diced red onion

1 small jalapeño chile, seeded and finely chopped

3 tablespoons chopped fresh cilantro leaves

2 tablespoons fresh lime juice

*1 tablespoon **each** red wine vinegar and honey*

Salt to taste

Ground white pepper to taste

Directions

1. In medium bowl, combine all ingredients.

2. Cover and refrigerate at least 1 hour to allow flavors to blend.

Makes 3 cups

Pineapple Citrus Relish

This combination of sweet and hot is especially good with grilled poultry or fish.

Ingredients

2 small juice oranges

2 cups fresh pineapple, diced into ½-inch pieces

1 medium red bell pepper, diced into ¼-inch pieces

2 green onions, thinly sliced (including green)

1 serrano chile, seeded and finely chopped

1 tablespoon chopped fresh cilantro leaves

1 teaspoon ground cumin

2 tablespoons lime juice

Directions

1. With sharp paring knife peel skin and white membrane from oranges. Segment and chop.

2. In medium bowl, mix all ingredients.

3. Cover and refrigerate at least 2 hours to allow flavors to blend.

Makes about 3 cups

Western Barbecue Sauce

Brush this spicy sauce on meat or poultry during the final minutes of grilling for a tangy southwestern flavor.

Ingredients

3 tablespoons vegetable oil

1½ cups chopped onion

2 cloves garlic, finely chopped

1 cup catsup

½ cup red wine vinegar

⅓ cup lemon juice

*¼ cup **each** Worcestershire sauce and packed brown sugar*

4 teaspoons chili powder

2 teaspoons ground celery seeds

1 teaspoon ground cumin

Directions

1. In large heavy saucepan, heat oil over medium heat. Sauté onion and garlic until tender.

2. Add remaining ingredients; bring to boil. Reduce heat to low; simmer uncovered 30 minutes. Cool.

3. Sauce can be refrigerated several days in covered container.

Makes about 3½ cups

Chili Sauce

This sweet-and-sour tomato sauce bears little resemblance to commercial chili sauce. Use it for Santa Fe Fajitas (page 81) or with pot roast or grilled burgers.

Ingredients

5 to 6 medium tomatoes

*1 **each** large green bell pepper and onion, cut up*

½ large red bell pepper, cut up

½ large jalapeño chile, seeded

1 cup cider vinegar

¾ cup sugar

2 teaspoons salt

*¼ teaspoon **each** chili powder and ground cinnamon*

Directions

1. In food processor, coarsely chop tomatoes, peppers, onion, and chile.

2. In Dutch oven, combine chopped vegetables with remaining ingredients. Bring mixture to boil; reduce heat to low and simmer uncovered 1 hour. Cool.

3. Refrigerate sauce. Serve with grilled meats.

Makes about 8½ cups

Zucchini Tomato Relish

Roma tomatoes, also called Italian plum tomatoes, are good for sauces because they have more flesh and fewer seeds and juice than other varieties.

Ingredients

2 medium zucchini, cut into 1-inch matchsticks

¼ cup cider vinegar

1 tablespoon each brown sugar and chopped fresh cilantro leaves

1 tablespoon chopped fresh basil (or 1 teaspoon dried basil, crushed)

3 cloves garlic, finely chopped

Freshly ground pepper to taste

3 large Italian plum (Roma) tomatoes, chopped

½ cup diced red onion

Directions

1. In 1½-quart saucepan, heat 1 quart water to boiling. Blanch zucchini 2 minutes. Drain and rinse well with cold water. Drain well on paper towel.

2. In large bowl, combine vinegar, brown sugar, cilantro, basil, garlic, and pepper. Toss zucchini, tomatoes, and red onion with dressing.

3. Cover and refrigerate at least 2 hours to allow flavors to blend.

Makes 1 quart

Honey Jalapeño Mustard

A great addition to sandwiches, this mustard keeps well and makes a good homemade gift from the kitchen.

Ingredients

¼ cup plus 3 tablespoons ground (dry) yellow mustard

1 tablespoon black mustard seed

6 tablespoons cider vinegar

1 teaspoon (or more) honey

1 to 2 jalapeño chiles, seeded and finely chopped

1 small clove garlic, finely chopped

Directions

1. In small bowl, combine all ingredients. Stir until a smooth paste forms. Add more honey if a milder mustard is desired.

2. Cover tightly and refrigerate.

Makes about ¾ cup

Rosy Salsa Mayonnaise

This luscious rosy sauce complements grilled meats or shrimp. Use it on sandwiches with leftover fajita meat or with cold grilled vegetables.

Ingredients

2 large Italian plum (Roma) tomatoes, peeled, seeded, and cut up

2 green onions, cut into 1-inch pieces (including green)

2 tablespoons fresh cilantro leaves

½ small jalapeño chile, seeded and cut up

1 teaspoon cider vinegar

¼ teaspoon salt

1 cup prepared mayonnaise

Directions

1. In blender or food processor, blend tomatoes, onions, cilantro, and chile until finely chopped.

2. Add vinegar and salt. Blend 30 seconds longer.

3. In small bowl, stir tomato mixture into mayonnaise until well blended.

4. Cover and refrigerate.

Makes 1½ cups

Herb Butters

Use these herb butters with grilled meat or vegetables.

Ingredients

½ cup butter or margarine (1 stick), softened

1 tablespoon dry sherry

*1 teaspoon **each** dried basil and oregano leaves*

1 clove garlic, finely chopped

Dash cayenne pepper

Directions

1. In small mixing bowl or food processor, beat all ingredients until well blended.

2. Cover and let stand 2 hours at room temperature to allow flavors to blend.

3. Refrigerate. Or, place on plastic wrap, seal, and shape into logs; chill or freeze, then slice.

Makes about ½ cup

Variations

Sage Butter: Mix ½ cup softened butter or margarine, 1 teaspoon dried crumbled sage, and ¼ teaspoon ground nutmeg.

Thyme Butter: Mix ½ cup softened butter or margarine, ½ teaspoon **each** dried thyme leaves and ground cumin.

Cilantro Butter: Mix ½ cup softened butter or margarine, 1 tablespoon **each** chopped fresh cilantro leaves and lime juice, ¼ teaspoon hot pepper sauce, and 1 clove garlic (finely chopped).

Fajitas and Other Southwestern Entrées

Fajitas are often the main event in traditional southwestern meals. The practice of cooking meats, poultry, or seafood outdoors is basic to the culture and climate of the Southwest: the weather is warm most of the year, so people want to keep their kitchens cool and be outdoors in the cooler evening hours. The popularity of fajitas also stems from the abundant beef, pork, and lamb available in the Southwest (San Antonio Fajitas, Pork Fajitas in Red Chile Sauce, Lamb Fajitas). Poultry (Chicken Fajitas Yucatan, Fajita Kabobs with Zucchini and Pineapple) also plays a versatile part in southwestern entrées. Shrimp, usually brought up from the Gulf of Mexico, is a southwestern favorite, enhanced by grilling with sauces featuring chiles or other assertive flavors (Shrimp in Vera Cruz Salsa, San Carlos Shrimp Fajitas with Roasted Pepper Sauce). Beans and cheese can also be combined with grilled vegetables to create satisfying, savory vegetarian dishes (Grande Vegetarian Delight).

Deluxe Fajitas

This version of fajitas is probably the most popular.

Ingredients

Brewer's Marinade (see page 19)

2 lbs. beef skirt or flank steak, skinned and boned chicken (breasts or thighs), or turkey tenderloin

2 medium green and/or red bell peppers, halved and seeded

1 large Spanish onion

Warm flour tortillas

Guacamole

Salsas

Dairy sour cream

Fresh cilantro leaves

Directions

1. Prepare marinade. Cut beef steaks into 4 pieces. Place meat in large recloseable plastic bag with marinade. Seal and turn bag several times to coat meat. Marinate in refrigerator at least 4 hours or overnight, turning occasionally.

2. Remove meat from marinade (reserve marinade). Grill meat, onions, and peppers over medium coals 4 minutes, basting with marinade. Turn and cook 4 minutes longer for medium rare.

3. Thinly slice meat or poultry across grain, holding knife at slight angle. Cut onion slices in half and cut peppers in strips.

4. Serve meat or poultry, onion, and peppers wrapped in tortillas with desired condiments.

Makes 6 servings

San Antonio Fajitas

You can warm tortillas directly on a hot grill before filling them with meat, onion, and condiments. Just hold the tortillas with tongs and lay them on the grill for a few minutes, turning once.

Ingredients

Tex-Mex Marinade (see page 18)

2 lbs. beef steak of choice (see page 16)

12 to 18 green onions

Warm flour tortillas

Guacamole

Salsas

Pico de Gallo (see page 56)

Sliced jalapeño chiles

Dairy sour cream

Directions

1. Prepare marinade. Trim steaks as needed; place in large recloseable plastic bag with marinade. Seal and turn bag several times to coat meat. Marinate in refrigerator at least 4 hours or overnight.

2. Tie 8 green onions together with kitchen twine about 3 inches from roots to form brush. Remove meat from marinade (reserve marinade). Grill meat over medium coals, using green onion brush to baste with marinade. Cook to desired doneness; time will vary depending on type of steak (1-inch steaks take 15 to 20 minutes total).

3. Untie green onion brush; roll all 12 to 18 green onions in marinade. Lay onions on grill and cook until green tops are wilted, 3 to 5 minutes.

4. Thinly slice meat across grain. Serve wrapped in tortillas with onions and desired condiments.

Makes 6 servings

Fajitas al Carbon

To prepare this recipe like Texan *carnitas*, cut meat in 4-inch strips and deep-fry in 3 cups of hot vegetable oil.

Ingredients

Cowboy Marinade (see page 18)

2 lbs. beef steak of choice (see page 16)

5 small yellow onions, cut in half lengthwise

Warm flour tortillas

Guacamole

Beans

Fresh cilantro leaves

Salsas

Directions

1. Prepare marinade. Place trimmed steaks and marinade in large shallow baking dish. Turn steaks to coat. Lay onions, cut side down, in marinade next to meat.

2. Cover and refrigerate dish. Marinate at least 4 hours or overnight, turning meat occasionally.

3. Place onions on greased grill over medium coals. Cook about 8 minutes; turn.

4. Remove meat from marinade (reserve marinade). Place meat on grill; baste meat and onions with marinade.

5. Continue cooking onions until soft and browned, about 6 to 9 minutes longer.

6. Continue cooking meat until browned and to desired doneness, turning once; time will vary depending on type of steak (1-inch steaks take 15 to 20 minutes total).

7. Thinly slice meat across grain. Serve wrapped in tortillas with desired condiments and onions.

Makes 6 servings

Carne Asada (Grilled Steak)

A garlic-herb paste flavors the grilled beef in these fajitas.

Ingredients

¼ cup olive oil

6 large cloves garlic

2 tablespoons lime juice

2 teaspoons dried rosemary leaves

1½ teaspoons chili powder

½ teaspoon dried oregano leaves

¼ teaspoon ground cumin

2 lbs. beef steak of choice (see page 16)

3 medium onions, cut into ½-inch slices

2 tablespoons butter or olive oil (optional)

Warm flour or corn tortillas

Salsa

Guacamole

Directions

1. In blender or food processor, purée oil, garlic, lime juice, rosemary, chili powder, oregano, and cumin.

2. Rub both sides of steaks with garlic-herb paste.

3. Grill steaks and onions over medium coals until meat is medium rare, 12 to 15 minutes (turning once), and onions are tender, 15 to 20 minutes. Or, broil steaks 4 inches from heat source about 7 minutes per side; sauté onions in butter until tender.

4. Thinly slice meat across grain. Serve wrapped in tortillas with onions, salsa, and guacamole.

Makes 4 to 6 servings

Steaks with Scorpion Relish

Serve guacamole and sour cream to take some of the sting out of the "scorpion" chile relish. Watch out!

Ingredients

6 to 8 whole green Anaheim chiles, roasted and peeled (or 1 cup canned chopped green chiles)

3 to 4 jalapeño chiles, seeded

½ small onion

¼ cup fresh cilantro leaves

2 tablespoons white distilled or cider vinegar

3 cloves garlic

2 teaspoons olive oil

*6 (6 oz. **each**) beef tenderloins or rib-eye steaks (¾ to 1 inch thick), or 6 large chicken breasts, skinned and boned*

Warm flour tortillas

Guacamole

Dairy sour cream

Directions

1. In food processor or blender, purée chiles, onion, cilantro, vinegar, garlic, and oil.

2. In large shallow baking dish, arrange steaks. Rub chile relish on both sides of steaks; cover and refrigerate 2 to 4 hours.

3. Wipe relish off steaks and set aside in small saucepan. Heat large heavy skillet over high heat. Sear steaks 2 minutes on each side to seal in juices. Place meat on rack in broiler pan 4 inches from heat source; broil until desired doneness, about 5 minutes.

4. Heat relish in saucepan until very hot. Serve with steaks, along with tortillas, guacamole, and sour cream.

Makes 6 servings

Fajita Kabobs with Zucchini and Pineapple

By making kabobs threaded with pieces of meat, vegetable, and fruit, your meal is nearly complete. Just add rice or beans and tortillas, of course.

Ingredients

Tropical Marinade (see page 19)

2 lbs. beef tenderloin, boneless chuck steak, London broil, pork loin or tenderloin, turkey tenderloin, or venison, cut into ½ × 2-inch strips

2 medium zucchini

1 small (about 3 lbs.) pineapple

10 to 12 (12-inch) metal or bamboo skewers*

Warm flour tortillas

Salsas

Fresh cilantro leaves

Directions

1. Prepare marinade. Place meat or poultry strips in large recloseable plastic bag. Pour marinade into bag; seal and turn bag several times to coat meat. Marinate in refrigerator at least 4 hours or overnight, turning occasionally.

2. Cut zucchini crosswise into ½-inch rounds. Cut pineapple (unpeeled) crosswise into ½-inch slices. Cut each pineapple slice into quarters.

3. Remove meat from marinade (reserve marinade). Thread meat and zucchini alternately onto 6 to 8 skewers. Thread pineapple pieces flat onto remaining skewers.

4. Grill over medium coals, basting with marinade. Cook 4 to 5 minutes; turn.

5. Cook pineapple 1 to 2 minutes longer; remove from grill and keep warm.

6. Cook meat and zucchini 3 to 4 minutes longer, until desired doneness. Serve with pineapple, tortillas, salsas, and cilantro.

*If using bamboo skewers, soak in water 20 minutes to prevent burning.

Makes 6 servings

Sonoma Fajitas

Wine makes a good marinade base, both because its acidic nature helps tenderize meat and because its flavor is so wonderful!

Ingredients

3 lbs. beef steak (see page 16), venison, or pork tenderloin, cut into ½ × 3-inch strips

2 cups dry red wine

*½ cup **each** chopped onion and olive oil*

*¼ cup **each** orange juice, lemon juice, and red wine vinegar*

1 teaspoon grated orange peel

*¼ teaspoon **each** dried thyme and oregano leaves*

8 peppercorns

2 cloves garlic, crushed

2 bay leaves, crumbled

Tex-Mex Oil (see page 21) or vegetable oil

Warm flour tortillas

Salsas

Directions

1. Place meat in large recloseable plastic bag and add remaining ingredients. Seal and turn bag several times to mix and coat meat. Marinate in refrigerator at least 4 hours or overnight, turning occasionally.

2. Remove meat from marinade (reserve marinade). In large heavy skillet, heat enough oil to coat bottom of skillet over medium-high heat. Sauté meat until browned on all sides, 2 to 5 minutes, stirring constantly. Or, grill meat threaded on skewers or in grill basket, over medium coals, until desired doneness, 5 to 6 minutes per side, basting with marinade.

3. Serve wrapped in tortillas with salsas.

Makes 6 to 8 servings

Santa Fe Fajitas

The sweet-and-sour Chili Sauce gives tang and sauciness to these fajitas.

Ingredients

3 lbs. skirt or flank steak, trimmed and cut into 6 pieces

4 cups Chili Sauce (see page 67)

Warm flour tortillas

Sliced ripe avocado

Fresh cilantro leaves

Dairy sour cream

Directions

1. Place steak and Chili Sauce in large recloseable plastic bag. Seal and turn bag several times to coat meat. Marinate in refrigerator at least 4 hours or overnight, turning occasionally.

2. Remove meat from marinade (reserve marinade). Grill over medium coals, 12 to 15 minutes for medium rare, turning once. Thinly slice meat across grain.

3. In large saucepan, bring reserved marinade to boil. Serve grilled meat with Chili Sauce, tortillas, avocado, cilantro, and sour cream.

Makes 6 to 8 servings

Pork Fajitas in Red Chile Sauce

Pork simmered in red chile sauce is a favorite filling for burritos and chimichangas in the Southwest. I've simply altered the form of the pork and served it as fajitas.

Ingredients

3 lbs. boneless pork loin roast or pork tenderloin

12 large dried chiles Colorado (mixture of mild and hot)

2 cups boiling water

½ medium onion, cut up

2 cloves garlic

*2 teaspoons **each** ground cumin and salt*

1½ teaspoons dried oregano leaves

6 to 8 (12-inch) metal or bamboo skewers*

Warm flour tortillas

Salsas

Guacamole

Directions

1. Cut pork into ¾-inch slices, then into ½ × 3-inch strips. Place in large recloseable plastic bag.

2. Remove stems and seeds from chiles. Place on baking sheet and toast in 250° oven 3 to 4 minutes, turning frequently to prevent burning.

3. Place toasted chiles in large bowl and pour boiling water over them. Soak 30 minutes.

4. In food processor or blender, pour chiles, water, onion, garlic, cumin, salt, and oregano. Process until nearly smooth.

5. Pour red chile sauce over pork strips. Seal and turn bag several times to coat meat. Refrigerate at least 4 hours or overnight, turning occasionally.

6. Remove meat from chile sauce (reserve sauce). Thread equal amounts of pork strips onto skewers, weaving back and forth.

7. Place kabobs on greased grate over medium coals. Grill 10 to 12 minutes, turning once halfway through cooking time. Or, broil 6 inches from heat in 550° oven 10 to 12 minutes, turning once.

8. In small saucepan, heat chile sauce to boiling. Pour through metal strainer if smoother sauce is desired.

9. Serve grilled pork with chile sauce, tortillas, salsas, and guacamole.

*If using bamboo skewers, soak in water 20 minutes to prevent burning.

Makes 6 to 8 servings

Orange-Honey Fajitas

An orange-honey marinade results in a tender, slightly glazed meat; the sautéed onions provide a sweet accompaniment.

Ingredients

3 lbs. skinned and boned chicken breast, turkey breast tenderloins, or fresh pork, cut into 3-inch strips

1 cup fresh orange juice (about 3 medium oranges)

2 medium onions, thinly sliced

*¼ cup **each** honey and red wine vinegar*

1 tablespoon grated orange peel

2 cloves garlic, finely chopped

2 tablespoons olive oil

½ teaspoon dried thyme leaves, crushed

*¼ teaspoon **each** ground allspice and coriander*

1 bay leaf

6 (12-inch) metal or bamboo skewers*

Warm flour tortillas

Mexican Spiced Rice (see page 109)

Directions

1. Place poultry or meat in large recloseable plastic bag. Combine remaining ingredients in bag with poultry or meat. Seal and turn bag to mix well. Refrigerate at least 4 hours, turning occasionally.

2. Remove poultry or meat from bag. Thread equal amounts onto skewers, weaving meat back and forth (unless sautéeing poultry or meat is preferred). Reserve marinade and onions.

3. Place kabobs on greased grate over medium coals. Grill until no longer pink, about 10 minutes, turning once; brush with some of the reserved marinade. (To sauté instead, stir poultry or meat strips and ¼ cup marinade in large skillet over medium heat until no longer pink, about 3 to 6 minutes. Keep warm.)

4. Meanwhile, in large skillet, sauté onions with ¼ cup reserved marinade over medium heat until tender, about 8 minutes. Serve warm with poultry or meat strips, tortillas or Mexican Spiced Rice.

*If using bamboo skewers, soak in water 20 minutes to prevent burning.

Makes 4 to 6 servings

Lamb Fajitas

Papaya Jicama Relish (page 64) is a nice choice to accompany the lamb and melon.

Ingredients

2 lbs. butterflied leg of lamb or boneless lamb shoulder, cut into 2-inch strips

⅓ cup **each** red wine vinegar and vegetable oil

¼ cup chopped fresh mint leaves

4 cloves garlic, crushed

1 tablespoon **each** dry sherry and soy sauce

1 bay leaf, crumbled

1 large (about 3 lbs.) honeydew melon, peeled and cut into 1-inch pieces

8 (12-inch) metal or bamboo skewers*

Warm flour tortillas

Directions

1. Place lamb in large recloseable plastic bag. Add remaining ingredients, except melon. Seal and turn bag several times to mix and coat meat. Marinate in refrigerator at least 4 hours or overnight, turning occasionally.

2. Remove lamb from marinade (reserve marinade). Thread meat onto skewers alternating with pieces of melon.

3. Grill skewers over medium coals, turning once, until lamb is slightly charred on outside but still pink inside, about 10 minutes. Or, broil 3 to 4 inches from heat source 5 minutes per side. Baste with reserved marinade during cooking. Serve wrapped in tortillas.

*If using bamboo skewers, soak in water 20 minutes to prevent burning.

Makes 6 servings

Chicken Fajitas Yucatan

Mexico's Mayan Indians were the first to use achiote seeds, which give this marinade its distinctive flavor and color. Serve whole or sliced chicken breasts topped with Pineapple Citrus Relish (page 65).

Ingredients

1 tablespoon achiote seeds

½ cup boiling water

*½ cup **each** orange juice and either grapefruit juice or white distilled vinegar*

2 tablespoons lime juice

4 cloves garlic

1 teaspoon peppercorns

*¼ teaspoon **each** whole allspice, cumin seed, and coriander seed*

6 large chicken breast halves (about 2½ lbs.) or 2½ lbs. venison, pork, or turkey breast

Warm flour tortillas

Salsas

Dairy sour cream

Directions

1. In small bowl, combine achiote seeds and water. Soak until soft, about 3 hours.

2. In blender, purée achiote and soaking liquid, orange juice, grapefruit juice or vinegar, lime juice, garlic, and spices.

3. Place chicken and marinade in large recloseable plastic bag. Seal and turn bag several times to coat meat. Marinate in refrigerator at least 4 hours or overnight, turning occasionally.

4. Remove meat from marinade (discard marinade). Grill over medium coals until no longer pink, 15 to 20 minutes, turning once. Serve wrapped in tortillas with salsas and sour cream.

Makes 6 servings

Chicken in Pumpkin Seed Sauce

Pumpkin seed sauce, or *pipian* sauce, gets its delicate green color from a blend of green seeds, herbs, and chiles.

Ingredients

½ cup hulled, raw pumpkin seeds

¼ cup blanched slivered almonds

¼ teaspoon cumin seeds

½ small onion, cut up

1 clove garlic

1 can (4 oz.) chopped green chiles, undrained

½ cup packed parsley leaves (or ¼ cup fresh cilantro leaves)

2 cups chicken broth, divided

4 large chicken breast halves, skinned and boned (about ½ lb.), cut into 2½-inch strips

2 tablespoons olive oil

1 tablespoon lemon juice

Warm flour tortillas

Shredded lettuce

Chopped tomato

Dairy sour cream

Sliced avocado

Sliced jalapeños

Directions

1. In large skillet, toast pumpkin seeds, almonds, and cumin seeds over low heat, shaking pan, until almonds are golden brown.

2. In food processor or blender, grind toasted mixture. Add onion, garlic, chiles, parsley, and 1 cup broth. Blend until smooth. Set aside.

3. In large skillet, sauté chicken strips in olive oil over medium-high heat 1 minute. Pour sauce into skillet with remaining 1 cup broth and lemon juice.

4. Bring mixture to a boil, reduce heat to low, and simmer uncovered until sauce is thickened, about 25 minutes.

5. Serve chicken wrapped in tortillas with sauce; garnish with desired condiments, such as shredded lettuce, tomato, sour cream, sliced avocado, or sliced jalapeños.

Makes 4 servings

San Carlos Shrimp Fajitas with Roasted Pepper Compote

A beer marinade is really tasty with shrimp; shrimp can be boiled in beer, too, with spices.

Ingredients

*Metal or bamboo skewers**

2 lbs. medium shrimp, peeled and deveined

1 cup beer

⅓ cup lemon juice

4 tablespoons olive oil

4 cloves garlic, 2 of these crushed

5 medium red bell peppers

*2 tablespoons **each** balsamic or red wine vinegar and olive oil*

2 tablespoons fresh cilantro and/or basil leaves

Salt

Freshly ground pepper

Warm flour tortillas

Directions

1. Thread shrimp onto metal or bamboo skewers. In 13×9×2-inch baking dish, combine beer, lemon juice, 2 tablespoons olive oil and 2 cloves crushed garlic.

2. Lay skewers in baking dish, turning to coat. Cover and marinate in refrigerator 1 hour, turning occasionally.

3. Meanwhile, roast and peel peppers (page 12), catching any juices in small bowl. Seed and cut up.

4. In food processor, purée peppers and their juice, vinegar, 2 tablespoons olive oil, cilantro and/or basil, 2 cloves garlic, and salt and pepper to taste. Set aside.

5. Remove shrimp skewers from marinade (reserve marinade). Grill over hot coals (high heat) until just opaque, 3 to 4 minutes per side, basting occasionally. Or, place baking dish with skewers in marinade in 400° oven and bake about 8 minutes.

6. Stir shrimp into roasted pepper sauce. Serve wrapped in warm tortillas.

*If using bamboo skewers, soak in water 20 minutes to prevent burning.

Makes 4 to 6 servings

Fajita Stir-Fry over Tortilla Quail Nests

Be sure to toast and grind your own cumin seeds; the flavor of the sauce will be stronger and nuttier than commercially ground cumin.

Ingredients

1 lb. lean beef steak (about 1 inch thick), such as sirloin or top round, or pork tenderloin, boned chicken breast, or turkey tenderloin

¼ cup vegetable oil, divided

2 small onions, cut into ½-inch wedges

1 each small red and yellow bell peppers, stemmed, seeded, and cut into thin slivers

1 can (4 oz.) chopped green chiles, drained

1 can (2.25 oz.) sliced ripe olives, drained

12 cherry tomatoes, halved

Tex-Mex Sauce (see below)

Salt

Tortilla Quail Nests (see below) or 8 cups shredded lettuce

Fresh cilantro leaves

Directions

1. Trim any excess fat from meat; cut meat across grain into ⅛ × 3-inch strips.

2. In large skillet, heat 2 tablespoons oil over high heat. Stir-fry half of meat or poultry until lightly browned, 2 to 3 minutes. Remove meat and keep warm. Add 1 tablespoon oil and repeat with remaining meat.

3. To skillet add last 1 tablespoon oil, onions, and bell peppers; stir-fry 3 minutes. Add chiles and olives; stir-fry until hot, 2 to 3 minutes longer.

4. Return meat to skillet and add tomatoes and Tex-Mex Sauce; stir until boiling. Season to taste with salt.

5. Pile Tortilla Quail Nests or lettuce on 4 dinner plates. Spoon stir-fry on top and garnish with cilantro.

Makes 4 servings

Tex-Mex Sauce

Ingredients

2 tablespoons each cornstarch and Worcestershire sauce
1 teaspoon each toasted cumin seeds and ground cumin
3 cloves garlic (crushed)
¼ teaspoon cayenne pepper
¾ cup beef or chicken broth

Directions

Mix all ingredients together.

Tortilla Quail Nests

Stack 8 (6-inch) corn tortillas; cut in half. Slice tortillas crosswise into ⅛-inch strips. In large skillet heat ½ inch vegetable oil to 375°. Drop tortilla strips into oil in batches; stir until brown and crisp, about 1 minute. Lift out with slotted spoon; drain on paper towels. Can be done ahead and stored airtight overnight. Makes 8 cups.

Shrimp in Vera Cruz Salsa

Because shrimp is more delicate than meat or poultry, you only need to marinate it for 1 hour.

Ingredients

1½ lb. medium shrimp, peeled and deveined

¼ cup **each** lemon juice, clam juice, and dry sherry

1 tablespoon finely chopped fresh basil (or 1 teaspoon dried basil leaves)

3 tablespoons olive oil

¼ teaspoon **each** sugar and salt

Freshly ground pepper

Vera Cruz Salsa (see below)

Diced avocado

Dairy sour cream

Warm flour tortillas

Directions

1. Place shrimp in large recloseable plastic bag. Add lemon juice, clam juice, dry sherry, basil, olive oil, sugar, salt, and pepper to taste. Seal and turn bag several times to mix and coat shrimp. Marinate in refrigerator 1 hour.

2. Meanwhile, prepare Vera Cruz Salsa.

3. Pour shrimp and marinade in large skillet. Cook over medium heat until shrimp turn pink, 5 to 6 minutes. Drain.

4. Prepare Vera Cruz Salsa. Serve with shrimp, garnished with avocado and sour cream, wrapped in tortillas.

Makes 4 servings

Vera Cruz Salsa

Ingredients

4 Italian plum (Roma) tomatoes, diced into ¼-inch pieces

½ cup **each** green and yellow peppers diced into ¼-inch pieces

¼ cup **each** finely chopped fresh basil and parsley

16 pimiento-stuffed green olives, quartered

3 tablespoons drained capers

2 tablespoons lemon juice

2 cloves garlic, finely chopped

Hot pepper sauce to taste

Salt to taste

Directions

Combine all ingredients and mix well.

Grande Vegetarian Delight
(Large Vegetable Burritos)

To give more zing to the grilled vegetables, marinate them in seasoned vinegar (garlic, basil, tarragon, or balsamic) for 4 hours before grilling.

Ingredients

1 **each** medium green and red bell peppers and Anaheim chile

2 small zucchini

1 large red onion

Basting Oil (see below) or Tex-Mex Oil (see page 21)

4 (12-inch) flour tortillas, warmed

1 can (15 oz.) black beans, drained and warmed

1½ cups shredded Monterey Jack cheese

Fresh cilantro leaves

Guacamole

Pico de Gallo (see page 56)

Dairy sour cream

Salsas

Directions

1. Cut peppers and Anaheim chile in half and remove seeds. Cut zucchini in half lengthwise. Cut onion into ½-inch slices.

2. Brush vegetables generously with Basting Oil. Grill over medium coals until tender, turning occasionally: 15 to 20 minutes for onion; 12 to 15 minutes for peppers and chile; 8 to 12 minutes for zucchini.

3. Cut peppers and chile into thin strips and cut zucchini crosswise into ¼-inch slices.

4. To assemble burritos, divide beans among tortillas. Top with equal amounts of vegetables. Sprinkle with cheese and cilantro. Fold tortillas up to enclose filling and place seam-side down on individual plates. Garnish with desired condiments.

Makes 4 servings

Basting Oil

Ingredients

6 tablespoons olive oil

2 tablespoons chopped fresh cilantro leaves

½ teaspoon ground cumin

¼ teaspoon **each** dried red pepper flakes and garlic salt

Directions

Mix all ingredients together.

Fajita Nacho Tidbits

Here's a great way to use leftover cooked meat! Serve with a citrus and avocado salad.

Ingredients

1 can (16 oz.) pinto beans, undrained

½ lb. marinated and cooked meat or poultry, chopped

2 tablespoons finely chopped onion

½ teaspoon chili powder

¼ teaspoon ground cumin

2 tablespoons chopped green chiles

1 bag (14 oz.) unsalted corn tortilla chips

1½ cups shredded Monterey Jack cheese

Fresh cilantro leaves

Directions

1. In medium saucepan, combine beans, meat or poultry, onion, chili powder, and cumin. Mash mixture slightly with back of spoon. Stir in green chiles.

2. Simmer mixture over medium heat 10 minutes.

3. Heat oven to 475°. Arrange chips on 15×10×1-inch baking pan. Spoon bean mixture onto each chip. Sprinkle with cheese. Bake until cheese is melted, about 5 minutes.

4. Serve nachos hot, garnished with cilantro.

Makes 4 servings

Barbecued Chicken Fajita Enchiladas

These enchiladas are very different from most classic renditions—and I think they're even better!

Ingredients

1 lb. skinned and boned chicken thigh meat, cut into ½×2-inch strips

½ cup dry sherry

¼ cup chopped red onion

2½ tablespoons tomato paste

*1 teaspoon **each** chili powder and ground cumin*

1 clove garlic, crushed

1 tablespoon vegetable oil

12 (6-inch) flour tortillas

*2 cans (10 oz. **each**) green enchilada sauce*

3 cups shredded Co-Jack cheese

Dairy sour cream

Salsa Fresca (see page 57)

Stewed or refried beans

Directions

1. In small shallow baking dish, mix first seven ingredients. Cover and refrigerate at least 4 hours, stirring occasionally.

2. Heat oven to 350°. In large skillet, heat oil over medium-high heat. Sauté chicken-marinade mixture until chicken is no longer pink, about 4 minutes.

3. Wrap tortillas in damp dish towel. In bottom of 13×9×2-inch baking dish, spread ¾ cup of enchilada sauce.

4. Working with one tortilla at a time (keep others covered), spoon about 2 tablespoons chicken mixture down center of each tortilla and sprinkle with 1½ tablespoons cheese. Roll tortillas up tightly and place seam-side down in baking dish.

5. Pour remaining sauce over rolled tortillas. Sprinkle with remaining cheese. Bake uncovered until heated through and bubbly, about 30 minutes.

6. Serve with sour cream, Salsa Fresca, and beans.

Makes 6 servings

Fajita Chimichangas Maximo

"Chimis" are just deep-fried burritos. This version makes very large chimichangas; you can also make "mini" versions for appetizers. Tucson is the original home of the chimichanga.

Ingredients

*6 cups Pork Fajitas in Red Chile Sauce
(see page 82)*

1½ cups refried beans, warmed

½ cup sliced green onions (including green)

6 (12-inch) flour tortillas, warmed

Vegetable oil

Salsas

Guacamole

Dairy sour cream

Shredded lettuce

Shredded Co-Jack cheese

Directions

1. Working with one tortilla at a time (keep others warm), place 1 cup pork, ¼ cup beans, and 1 heaping tablespoon onions in center of bottom third of tortilla.

2. Fold bottom of tortilla up over filling, then fold over each side. Fold top down over filling and secure with toothpicks. (This can be done a day ahead; cover and refrigerate.)

3. In Dutch oven or deep-fryer, heat 3 inches oil to 375°. Fry each chimichanga until golden, about 4 to 6 minutes. Serve garnished as desired.

Makes 6 servings

Oven-Fried Chimichangas

Heat oven to 425°. Place chimichangas on a 15×10×1-inch baking pan. Brush both sides of each chimichanga with oil. Bake until golden, about 20 minutes, turning every 5 minutes.

Fajita Tostadas

These layered tostadas are a deluxe version of cheese tostadas, a snack food in the Southwest.

Ingredients

1½ lbs. marinated and cooked chicken, turkey, or pheasant, cut into 1½ × ½-inch strips

1 can (4 oz.) chopped green chiles, undrained

½ cup dairy sour cream

¼ cup finely chopped red onion

Vegetable oil

6 (7-inch) flour tortillas

1½ cups refried beans, warmed

2 cups shredded iceberg lettuce

1 can (2.25 oz.) sliced ripe olives, drained

1½ cups shredded sharp Cheddar cheese

¼ cup fresh cilantro leaves

Guacamole

Salsa

Directions

1. In medium bowl, mix poultry strips, chiles, sour cream, and onion. Set aside.

2. In large skillet, heat ½ inch oil over medium heat. Fry tortillas, one at a time, until lightly browned and blistered, about 30 seconds per side. Drain on paper towels. Keep warm.

3. To assemble each tostada, spread with ¼ cup beans, then layer with lettuce, poultry mixture, olives, cheese, and cilantro. Serve with guacamole and salsa.

Makes 4 servings

Gringo Tacos

These grilled tacos are a fancier version of *quesadillas*.

Ingredients

8 (6- to 7-inch) flour tortillas, warmed

1 cup refried beans or Spicy Black Beans with Goat Cheese (see page 114), warmed

1½ lbs. marinated and cooked meat or poultry, thinly sliced

1 small ripe avocado, peeled and thinly sliced

1½ cups shredded Co-Jack cheese

Salsa

Dairy sour cream

Fresh cilantro leaves

Directions

1. Spread each tortilla with thin layer of beans. Layer with meat slices, avocado, and cheese.

2. Fold tortillas in half. Grill on lightly greased griddle over medium heat until both sides are lightly browned, 1 to 2 minutes. Or, place in grill basket or directly on greased grill over medium coals. Serve with salsa, sour cream, and cilantro.

Makes 4 servings

Fajita Tacos

The flavor of these tacos made with fajita meat beats that of tacos made with ground meat hands down!

Ingredients

2 lbs. marinated and grilled or broiled steak of choice

Vegetable oil

12 (6-inch) corn tortillas or crisp taco shells

2 medium tomatoes, chopped

1 medium onion, chopped

1 large avocado, pitted and diced

2 cups shredded lettuce

1½ cups shredded sharp Cheddar cheese

Tomatillo Salsa (see page 62) or commercial green taco sauce

Directions

1. Thinly slice steak across grain. Keep warm.

2. In large skillet, heat ½ inch oil over medium heat. Dip each tortilla into oil and fry until soft and pliable, about 15 seconds. Drain and fold in half. Keep warm.

3. To assemble tacos, fill each fried tortilla or taco shell with sliced meat, tomato, onion, avocado, lettuce, and cheese. Top with salsa.

Makes 12 tacos (4 to 6 servings)

Fajita-Stuffed Potatoes

This is a great, quick way to use leftover fajita meat. It's even faster if you can microwave the potatoes.

Ingredients

*4 large russet potatoes (6 to 7 oz. **each**), scrubbed*

1 lb. marinated and grilled meat or poultry of choice, thinly sliced

1 cup thick tomato salsa

*¼ cup **each** chopped green pepper and sliced green onion (including green)*

¼ cup butter or margarine (optional)

Salt

Freshly ground pepper

Dairy sour cream

Fresh cilantro leaves

Directions

1. Heat oven to 350°. Bake potatoes until tender, about 1 hour. Or, microwave according to directions for your oven.

2. In medium bowl, mix meat or poultry strips, salsa, green pepper, and onion.

3. Split potatoes. Fluff with fork and stir 1 tablespoon butter or margarine into each potato, if desired. Season to taste with salt and pepper.

4. Top each potato with one quarter of meat or poultry mixture. Garnish with sour cream and cilantro.

Makes 4 servings

Enchilada Stack Suiza

"Swiss" enchiladas, made with a cheese sauce, are available in restaurants throughout the Southwest. A stacked version cuts down the work somewhat—they're worth the effort!

Ingredients

¼ cup butter or margarine, divided

½ cup chopped onion

2 cloves garlic, finely chopped

½ cup chopped red bell pepper

1 jalapeño chile, seeded and chopped

1 package (10 oz.) frozen chopped spinach, thawed and squeezed dry

1 cup chopped or shredded chicken or turkey, grilled or sautéed

1½ teaspoons dried oregano leaves, crushed

1 tablespoon all-purpose flour

1 cup milk

1 cup dairy sour cream

1½ cups **each** shredded Longhorn Cheddar and Monterey Jack cheese (or 3 cups shredded Co-Jack cheese), divided

8 (6-inch) blue or yellow corn tortillas

Sliced avocado

Green onions, sliced (including green)

Cherry tomato halves

Directions

1. In large skillet, melt 3 tablespoons butter or margarine over medium heat. Sauté onion, garlic, bell pepper, and jalapeño until tender, about 5 minutes. Stir in spinach, poultry, and oregano; cook 3 minutes longer. Set aside.

2. In medium saucepan, melt 1 tablespoon butter or margarine over low heat. Stir in flour and cook until golden, about 4 minutes, stirring constantly. Whisk in milk and cook until thickened. Stir in sour cream and 1¼ cups **each** Cheddar and Monterey Jack cheeses (or 2½ cups Co-Jack), stirring until melted and sauce is smooth.

3. Pour ¾ cup cheese sauce into spinach mixture. Reserve remaining sauce.

4. Heat oven to 375°. Grease 9-inch glass pie plate or round gratin dish.

5. Dip 1 tortilla into cheese sauce; place in dish. Top with about ½ cup spinach mixture. Repeat with remaining tortillas and filling. Top stacked tortillas with remaining ½ cup shredded cheese.

6. Bake uncovered until stack is heated through and cheese is melted and bubbly, about 20 minutes. Garnish as desired and cut stack in wedges (quarters).

Makes 4 servings

Grilled Fajita Salad

Nopales, the pads of the prickly pear cactus, are most often used in salads. Their flavor is similar to green beans.

Ingredients

1 lb. marinated and grilled strips of skirt or flank steak, chicken breast, venison, or pork

8 red new potatoes, cooked and sliced, not peeled

1 jar (15 oz.) nopalitos, drained and rinsed (cut into strips if not already cut)

12 cherry tomatoes, halved

Rosemary Vinaigrette (see below)

8 cups shredded fresh spinach

4 green onions, sliced (including green)

1 cup crumbled Cotija cheese, aged Goat cheese, or fresh Parmesan cheese

Directions

1. In large bowl, combine meat or poultry strips, potatoes, nopalitos, and tomatoes. Toss with half of Rosemary Vinaigrette. Cover and refrigerate 2 hours.

2. Divide spinach among four plates. Top each plate with one-fourth of meat mixture. Drizzle with remaining dressing; sprinkle with green onions and cheese.

Makes 4 servings

Rosemary Vinaigrette

Ingredients

¼ cup red wine vinegar

1 tablespoon Dijon-style mustard

1 clove garlic, crushed

1 teaspoon dried rosemary leaves, crushed

Directions

1. In small bowl, combine first four ingredients.

2. Whisk in oil.

Topopo Salad Bowls

You can even eat the bowl of these Mexican-style chef salads!

Ingredients

8 cups shredded lettuce

2 cups cooked bay shrimp, diced cooked chicken, or turkey

2 medium tomatoes, diced

1 medium red onion, thinly sliced

½ cup frozen corn and/or peas, thawed

8 radishes, sliced

1 can (2.25 oz.) sliced ripe olives, drained

Cilantro Vinaigrette (see below)

1⅓ cups refried beans, warmed

Tortilla Bowls (see below)

2 cups shredded Longhorn Cheddar cheese

Guacamole

Salsa

Directions

1. In large bowl, combine lettuce, shrimp or poultry, tomatoes, onion, corn and/or peas, radishes, and olives. Pour Cilantro Vinaigrette over mixture and toss well.

2. Spread ⅓ cup beans in bottom of each Tortilla Bowl. Divide salad mixture evenly among bowls. Top each with ½ cup cheese. Serve with guacamole and salsa.

Makes 4 servings

Cilantro Vinaigrette

Ingredients

¾ cup olive oil

½ cup lime juice

¼ cup chopped fresh cilantro leaves

1 teaspoon dry mustard

1 clove garlic, crushed

⅛ teaspoon cayenne pepper

Directions

In small bowl, whisk all ingredients together.

Tortilla Bowls

Directions

In Dutch oven or deep-fryer, heat 5 inches vegetable oil to 375°. Have 4 (12-inch) flour tortillas on hand. Remove bottom of empty 28-oz. can with can opener to form open-ended cylinder. Place 1 tortilla in hot oil. Holding edge of can with tongs, press down on center of tortilla; edge of tortilla will curve up to form bowl. Fry until lightly browned and crisp, about 1 minute; tilt tortilla to fry top edge. Remove can and tortilla from oil; carefully pull can away from tortilla if attached. Drain on paper towels. Repeat with remaining tortillas.

Marinated Steak Fajita Sandwiches

Cilantro Spread is really an adaptation of an Italian pesto sauce, with cilantro substituted for the traditional basil.

Ingredients

1 lb. flank steak, marinated in marinade of choice

1 tablespoon butter or margarine

1 medium red onion, sliced

Cilantro Spread (see below) or Rosy Salsa Mayonnaise (see page 70)

4 long French rolls or large onion rolls, split

1 can (16 oz.) refried beans

1⅓ cups shredded Longhorn Cheddar cheese

Directions

1. Grill or sauté steak. Thinly slice across grain. Keep warm.

2. In medium skillet, melt butter or margarine over medium-high heat. Sauté onion until tender, about 8 minutes. Set aside.

3. Spread bottoms of rolls with Cilantro Spread or Rosy Salsa Mayonnaise. Layer with meat, onion, beans, and cheese. Place on baking sheet.

4. Broil sandwiches 4 to 6 inches from heat source until cheese is melted.

5. Spread tops of rolls with spread of choice and place on sandwiches.

Makes 4 servings

Cilantro Spread

Ingredients

¾ cup fresh cilantro leaves, packed

¼ cup grated Parmesan cheese

2 tablespoons pine nuts

1 clove garlic

6 tablespoons olive oil

Directions

1. In blender or food processor, purée first four ingredients.

2. Gradually blend in oil.

Fajita Pockets

Serve these pita sandwiches with Citrus Tomato Gazpacho for a light meal.

Ingredients

2 large pita bread rounds

Honey Jalapeño Mustard (see page 69) or Dijon-style mustard

2 cups shredded fresh spinach

1 lb. meat or poultry strips, marinated and grilled or sautéed

1 cup chopped tomato

4 slices bacon, fried crisp and crumbled

Guacamole

Directions

1. Cut each pita round in half. Spread inside of each pocket with mustard.

2. Fill each pocket, dividing spinach, meat or poultry strips, tomato, and bacon evenly. Serve with guacamole.

Makes 2 to 4 servings

Quick Black Bean Chili

It's not always necessary to simmer chili for hours to get a savory, rich stew.

Ingredients

¼ lb. bulk chorizo or hot Italian sausage

1½ cups chopped onion

4 cloves garlic, finely chopped

1 jalapeño chile, seeded and finely chopped

2 tablespoons ground hot red chile

1 tablespoon ground cumin

1 can (28 oz.) Italian plum (Roma) tomatoes, chopped, juice reserved

¼ cup bourbon

1 tablespoon dried oregano leaves, crushed

½ teaspoon ground cinnamon

1 can (15 oz.) black beans, rinsed and drained

¼ cup tomato paste

1 lb. marinated and grilled or sautéed beef, pork, or venison, cut into ½-inch cubes

1 tablespoon red wine vinegar

Salt

Freshly ground pepper

Grated Asiago or Fontina cheese

Directions

1. In Dutch oven, brown sausage and drain, reserving fat. Set sausage aside.

2. Sauté onion and garlic in fat over low heat until tender, about 10 minutes. Increase heat to medium; add jalapeño, ground chile, and cumin. Cook and stir 5 minutes.

3. Stir in sausage, tomatoes, reserved juice, bourbon, oregano, and cinnamon. Reduce heat to low, cover, and simmer for 30 minutes, stirring occasionally.

4. Stir in beans, tomato paste, and meat strips. Simmer 5 minutes. Stir in vinegar and season to taste with salt and pepper. Serve topped with cheese.

Makes 6 servings

Side Dishes

(Tortillas, Beans, Rice, and Vegetables)

Tortillas, beans, and rice, staples of the Southwest, are rarely missing from southwestern meals. Tortillas are the basis of every meal, whether served as a bread or as an integral part of the entrée. And the fire-quenching effect of beans and rice makes them a natural accompaniment to spicy main courses (Mexican Spiced Rice, Arroz Verde, Stewed Garbanzos, Spicy Black Beans with Goat Cheese). Vegetables round out any menu, providing color, flavor, and balance (New Mexican Calabacitas, Barbecue Roasted Corn with Cumin Butter, Acapulco Vegetable Ragout).

Flour Tortillas

Tortilla dough needs to rest to allow the gluten in the flour to relax so the dough will roll out easily. Lard is the traditional fat used for flour tortillas, but vegetable shortening is a healthier alternative.

Ingredients

2 cups all-purpose or unbleached flour

1 teaspoon salt

3 tablespoons shortening or lard

½ cup water

Directions

1. In large bowl, combine flour and salt. Cut in shortening or lard with pastry blender or fork until particles are size of small peas.

2. Sprinkle with water, 2 tablespoons at a time, until all flour is moistened and dough begins to form ball when mixed. Gather dough into ball; divide into 12 equal parts. Shape into balls and brush with shortening. Cover and let rest 20 minutes.

3. On lightly floured surface, roll each ball into 6- or 7-inch circle. Cook on ungreased hot griddle or skillet over medium-high heat until tortilla is dry around edges and blisters appear on surface, about 2 minutes. Turn and cook other side until dry, 1 minute longer. Tortillas can be stacked with wax paper between each; refrigerate in recloseable plastic bag.

Makes 12 (6- to 7-inch) tortillas

Corn Tortillas

Don't substitute corn meal for masa harina—it's much coarser. Blue corn masa is available from New Mexico, but it's more difficult to work with and tends to make a crumblier dough.

Ingredients

2 cups masa harina

1¼ cups water

24 (7-inch) squares waxed paper

Tortilla press (optional)

Directions

1. In large bowl, mix masa and water until well blended and dough begins to form ball. Gather dough into ball; divide into 12 equal parts. Cover and let rest 10 minutes.

2. To roll tortillas by hand, place each ball on a waxed paper square. Cover with second waxed paper square, flattening ball slightly. Roll into 6-inch circle. Or, put 1 waxed paper square on bottom half of tortilla press. Place ball of dough on press, slightly off center, toward edge opposite handle. Flatten ball slightly and cover with second waxed paper square. Lower top of press and press down firmly on lever until tortilla is about 6 inches in diameter. Remove tortilla, keeping it between paper, and repeat with remaining dough.

3. Peel off top piece of waxed paper and carefully invert each tortilla on ungreased griddle or skillet; cook over medium-high heat until dry around edge, about 1 minute. Remove second piece of waxed paper and turn tortilla, cooking until dry, about 2 minutes. Stack tortillas with fresh waxed paper between each. Store in refrigerator in recloseable plastic bag.

Makes 12 (6-inch) tortillas

Brown Rice with Cilantro and Pine Nuts

The fresh flavors of lemon peel and cilantro blend well with brown rice and rich pine nuts.

Ingredients

2¼ cups water

1 cup long-grain brown rice

2 teaspoons chicken bouillon granules

2 tablespoons toasted pine nuts (see page 3)

1 tablespoon chopped fresh cilantro leaves

1 teaspoon grated lemon peel

Directions

1. In 1-quart saucepan, combine water, rice, and bouillon. Bring mixture to boiling; reduce heat to low, cover, and simmer 40 minutes.

2. Remove from heat and let stand 5 minutes. Uncover, fluff with fork, and stir in pine nuts, cilantro, and lemon peel.

Makes 4 servings

Mexican Spiced Rice

A touch of spices and raisins gives this rice a subtle sweetness that compliments spicy-hot foods.

Ingredients

2 tablespoons butter or margarine

½ cup chopped onion

*¼ cup **each** diced carrot and celery*

1½ cups long-grain white rice

2 teaspoons ground cinnamon

½ teaspoon anise seeds

3 cups chicken broth

½ cup raisins or currants

Directions

1. In 1½-quart saucepan, melt butter or margarine over medium heat. Sauté onion, carrot, and celery until tender, about 10 minutes, stirring occasionally.

2. Stir rice, cinnamon, and anise seeds into vegetable mixture. Pour in broth, cover pan, and simmer over low heat 20 minutes.

3. Stir in raisins or currants with fork, fluffing rice. Cover and let stand 5 minutes. Serve hot.

Makes 6 servings

Spanish Rice

Rice is always served alongside fajitas—this style is a perennial favorite.

Ingredients

1 tablespoon olive oil

1 medium onion, chopped

1 clove garlic, finely chopped

1½ cups long-grain white rice

2 teaspoons chili powder

1 can (16 oz.) whole tomatoes, chopped, juice reserved

2 teaspoons chicken bouillon granules

½ teaspoon salt

1 cup frozen peas, thawed

2 tablespoons chopped pimiento

Directions

1. In 2-quart saucepan, heat oil over medium heat. Sauté onion and garlic until tender.

2. Stir in rice, chili powder, and tomatoes until well mixed.

3. Pour reserved tomato juice into 4-cup glass measuring cup. Add water until liquid level equals 3 cups.

4. Pour liquid mixture, bouillon, and salt into saucepan, stirring well.

5. Bring mixture to boiling, reduce heat to low, cover, and simmer 20 minutes. Remove from heat and let stand 5 minutes longer.

6. Uncover; gently stir peas and pimiento into rice with fork. Serve hot.

Makes 6 servings

Arroz Verde

This creamy green rice is a soothing side dish to serve with a spicy entree.

Ingredients

1 cup long-grain white rice

2 cups water

½ teaspoon salt

1 tablespoon vegetable oil

½ cup chopped green onion (including green)

1 clove garlic, finely chopped

4 poblano or Anaheim chiles, roasted, peeled, and chopped or 1 can (4 oz.) diced green chiles, drained

½ cup dairy sour cream

¼ cup chopped fresh cilantro leaves

1½ cups shredded white Cheddar cheese

Directions

1. In 1-quart saucepan, bring rice, water, and salt to boiling. Reduce heat to low, cover, and simmer until rice is tender and all water is absorbed, 20 to 25 minutes. Transfer rice to medium bowl and cool, fluffing occasionally with fork.

2. Heat oven to 325°. Grease 1½-quart shallow baking dish.

3. In small skillet, heat oil over medium heat. Sauté onion and garlic 2 minutes. Stir in chiles and cook 1 minute longer.

4. Mix onion mixture into rice. Stir sour cream and cilantro together, then into rice. Stir in cheese.

5. Transfer rice mixture to prepared baking dish. Bake until edges are light brown and mixture is heated through, about 25 minutes.

Makes 4 to 6 servings

Borracho Beans

These "drunken" pintos are a great alternative to refried beans. Use a dark Mexican beer to give a heartier flavor—my favorite is Dos Equis.

Ingredients

1 lb. dried pinto beans, sorted and rinsed

4½ cups beef broth

*2 bottles (12 oz. **each**) dark beer*

1½ cups chopped onion

4 cloves garlic, finely chopped

½ lb. bacon (preferably mesquite-smoked), cut into 1-inch pieces

2 medium red bell peppers, roasted, peeled, and chopped

2 jalapeño chiles, seeded and finely chopped

2 teaspoons salt

Directions

1. In large bowl, place beans and add boiling water to cover beans 2 inches deep. Soak 30 minutes. Drain any excess water.

2. In Dutch oven, place soaked beans, broth, beer, onion, and garlic. Bring mixture to boil. Reduce heat, cover, and simmer 1 hour, stirring occasionally.

3. Meanwhile, in medium skillet, cook bacon over medium heat until brown and crisp, about 15 minutes, stirring occasionally. Drain well on paper towels.

4. After beans have simmered 1 hour, stir in bacon, bell peppers, jalapeños and salt.

5. Cover and continue to simmer beans until just tender, about 1 hour longer, stirring often. Serve with slotted spoon.

Makes 6 to 8 servings

Rancho Refried Beans

The beans can be mashed in a food processor, if desired, before refrying.

Ingredients

5 tablespoons olive oil

1 cup chopped onion

3 cloves garlic, finely chopped

1 tablespoon ground hot red chile

*1 teaspoon **each** ground coriander, ground cumin, dried oregano leaves (crushed), and salt*

¼ teaspoon ground cinnamon

*2 cans (16 oz. **each**) pinto beans, undrained, or 3 cups freshly cooked pinto beans with some cooking liquid*

Shredded cheese (optional)

Sliced green onion (optional)

Directions

1. In large skillet, heat oil over medium heat. Sauté onion and garlic until tender, about 6 minutes. Stir in ground chile, coriander, cumin, oregano, salt, and cinnamon.

2. Reduce heat to low. Add beans with liquid (about ½ cup) and mash with potato masher. Cook beans until mixture is quite thick but still moist, about 30 to 40 minutes, stirring occasionally. If beans get too dry, add a little water. Beans should be slightly crisp around edges.

3. Sprinkle with cheese and onion, if desired.

Makes 6 servings

Spicy Black Beans with Goat Cheese

If you can find fresh epazote (an herb from Mexico), use it to give black beans a distinctive flavor. Some claim it even reduces their flatulence-causing properties! Serve this dish as an accompaniment to fajitas or other southwestern entrées or as an appetizer with chips.

Ingredients

*1 lb. dried black beans, sorted and rinsed or 3 cans (16 oz. **each**) black beans*

3 quarts water

5 cloves garlic, crushed

2 tablespoons dry mustard

1 tablespoon chopped fresh epazote leaves (optional)

2 teaspoons cumin seeds, toasted and ground (divided)

1 teaspoon dried oregano leaves, crushed (divided)

Salt

2 jalapeño chiles, seeded and finely chopped

8 oz. mild soft goat cheese

4 green onions, sliced (including green)

Directions

1. If using dried beans, place beans in Dutch oven and cover with boiling water by 3 inches. Let stand 2 hours; drain. If using canned beans, proceed to step 3.

2. Pour 3 quarts water over soaked beans. Add garlic, mustard, epazote, 1 teaspoon cumin, and ½ teaspoon oregano. Bring mixture to boil, reduce heat to low, cover, and simmer until beans mash easily, about 2 hours.

3. Drain beans, reserving liquid. Salt beans to taste. Mash beans, adding liquid as needed to keep beans moist. For home-cooked beans, stir in remaining 1 teaspoon cumin, ½ teaspoon oregano, and jalapeños. If using canned beans, stir in 3 cloves finely chopped garlic; 1½ teaspoons **each** dried mustard, epazote, and cumin; 1 teaspoon oregano; jalapeños.

4. Heat oven to 350°. Grease 3-quart shallow baking dish. Spoon beans into dish and crumble cheese on top. Bake 15 minutes. Sprinkle with onions.

Makes 10 to 12 servings

Stewed Garbanzo Beans

Serve these garbanzos as an alternative to pinto or refried beans.

Ingredients

6 slices bacon or ½ lb. bulk chorizo sausage

1 cup chopped onion

1 clove garlic, finely chopped

*2 cans (15 oz. **each**) garbanzo beans (chickpeas), rinsed and drained*

3 tablespoons ground red chile (or to taste)

½ teaspoon dried oregano leaves, crushed

¼ teaspoon ground cumin

Salt

1 tablespoon chopped fresh cilantro leaves (optional)

Directions

1. In medium skillet, fry bacon until crisp, or brown chorizo. Drain, reserving 2 tablespoons fat. Crumble bacon; set aside.

2. Sauté onion and garlic in fat until tender.

3. In large saucepan, combine beans, onion mixture, red chile, oregano, cumin, and salt to taste. Simmer mixture over low heat until hot.

4. Stir in bacon or chorizo and cilantro, if desired. Serve hot.

Makes 6 servings

Grilled Fresh Vegetables

Vegetable kabobs, with all pieces cut the same size, will cook for 10 to 15 minutes. Refrigerate any leftover vegetables and serve later as a salad with Rosy Salsa Mayonnaise (page 70). To reheat vegetables, spread on 15×10×1-inch baking pan and heat at 350° for 7 to 10 minutes.

Ingredients

Choice of vegetables (see chart below)

Tex-Mex Oil (see page 21), or Herb Butters (see page 71), or seasoned or flavored vinegars

Directions

1. Choose one or several fresh vegetables. Allow 2 to 3 whole vegetables per serving.

2. Coat vegetables with Tex-Mex Oil or Herb Butters, or soak in seasoned vinegar, 1 hour before grilling. Place vegetables directly on grill or in grill basket, over medium coals. Cook, turning often and brushing with oil or butter as needed to keep moist, until the vegetables are tender and brown grill marks appear (see chart below for time ranges).

3. Serve hot or at room temperature.

Makes as much as desired

Vegetables for Grilling

Vegetables	Preparation	Grill Time
Onions (yellow or red)	½-inch slices	15 to 20 minutes
Green Onions	Trim, cook whole	5 minutes
Summer Squash (zucchini, pattypan, or yellow crookneck)	Slice or halve lengthwise	8 to 12 minutes
Potatoes (russet or sweet)	½-inch slices	14 to 16 minutes
Bell Peppers (green, red, yellow)	Halve lengthwise and remove seeds	12 to 15 minutes
Mushrooms	Thread on skewers whole	12 to 14 minutes
Eggplant (small or Oriental)	Slice lengthwise into ¾-inch wedges or halve Oriental lengthwise	10 to 12 minutes
Cherry Tomatoes	Thread on skewers whole	About 5 minutes

Grilled Whole Green Chiles

Grilled or roasted green chiles, peeled and cut in strips, are a popular southwestern side dish called *rajas*.

Ingredients

6 large, fresh, mild green chiles (Anaheim or poblano)

Directions

1. On lightly greased grill, place chiles 4 to 6 inches above hot coals.

2. Cook uncovered until chiles are blistered and slightly charred, about 2 to 3 minutes, turning once. Remove from heat.

3. Peel any blistered skin that comes off easily. Serve whole. If desired, slit each chile lengthwise and scrape out seeds before serving.

Makes 3 to 6 servings

New Mexican Calabacitas (Zucchini Sauté)

For a different presentation, serve calabacitas in green or red bell pepper cups, hollowed tomatoes, or corn husk "boats" (page 8).

Ingredients

1 tablespoon olive oil

½ cup chopped onion

1 clove garlic, finely chopped

2 medium zucchini, diced into ½-inch pieces (1½ cups)

1 cup fresh or frozen whole corn kernels

½ cup diced tomato (½-inch pieces)

1 tablespoon chopped fresh cilantro leaves

Salt and hot pepper sauce

Directions

1. In large skillet, heat oil over medium heat. Sauté onion and garlic 2 minutes.

2. Stir in zucchini and corn. Cook 5 minutes longer.

3. Add tomato and cilantro and cook until heated through.

4. Season to taste with salt and hot pepper sauce. Serve hot or at room temperature.

Makes 4 to 6 servings

Barbecue Roasted Corn with Cumin Butter

If you prefer to cook the corn inside, simmer the ears in a large kettle of boiling water for 10 minutes. Corn can be cut into 2-inch pieces and marinated in your favorite salsa at room temperature for a colorful side dish.

Ingredients

4 ears fresh corn

¼ cup butter or margarine

½ teaspoon ground cumin

¼ teaspoon garlic salt

⅛ teaspoon ground hot red chile or cayenne pepper

1 tablespoon finely chopped fresh cilantro leaves

Directions

1. Remove large outer husks of corn. Turn back inner husks and remove all silk. Replace inner husks over ears and soak ears in cold water 1 hour. Remove from water and shake off excess. Grill over hot coals until tender, 15 to 30 minutes, turning frequently. Or, husk ears completely (do not soak) and grill directly on outer edge of lightly oiled grate over hot coals until tender, 15 to 20 minutes, turning frequently.

2. In small saucepan, melt butter over low heat. Stir in cumin, garlic salt, and hot chile or cayenne pepper. Remove from heat and stir in cilantro. Brush on corn before serving.

Makes 4 servings

Garlic Roasted Potato Spears

These oven-crisp wedges are better than french fries!

Ingredients

3 tablespoons olive oil

4 cloves garlic, crushed

4 large russet potatoes, scrubbed

Salt

Lemon-pepper seasoning

Paprika

Directions

1. Heat oven to 350°. Grease 15×10×1-inch baking pan.

2. In small bowl, mix oil and garlic; set aside.

3. Cut potatoes in half crosswise, then lengthwise into eighths (each potato will yield 16 spears).

4. Arrange spears skin-side down on prepared pan. Brush each spear with oil-garlic mixture. Salt spears to taste, then sprinkle generously with lemon-pepper seasoning and paprika until well coated.

5. Bake until golden and crisp, about 1 hour. Serve hot.

Makes 4 to 6 servings

Grilled Potato Packet

Cooking food in a foil packet on the grill is easy; try your own combinations of sliced vegetables and seasonings. Vegetables are done when tender, so adjust cooking time accordingly.

Ingredients

3 large russet potatoes, scrubbed and thinly sliced

1½ cups thinly sliced onion

2 tablespoons olive oil

2 teaspoons fresh rosemary (or 1 teaspoon dried rosemary, crushed)

Salt

Freshly ground pepper

Directions

1. Cut 2 large squares of aluminum foil; grease one side of each square.

2. Layer potatoes and onion on 1 foil square. Drizzle with oil and sprinkle with rosemary. Season to taste with salt and pepper.

3. Cover potato mixture with second square of foil (greased side down); seal edges well.

4. Place foil packet on grill over medium-hot coals. Cook until vegetables are tender, about 45 minutes.

Makes 4 servings

Caramelized Onions

Sautéing onions slowly brings out their delicate sweetness. The golden brown strands of caramelized onions are just about the best accompaniment I know for grilled meats. Browning is caused by the caramelization of natural sugars in the onions.

Ingredients

3 tablespoons butter or margarine

6 cups thinly sliced red onions (about 6 medium)

Salt

Freshly ground pepper

Directions

1. In large heavy-bottomed skillet or Dutch oven, melt butter over low heat.

2. Add onions and cook slowly until soft and dark golden brown, about 30 minutes, stirring occasionally.

3. Season to taste with salt and pepper. Serve warm with grilled or broiled meat.

Makes 6 servings

Acapulco Vegetable Ragout (Stew)

A stew of colorful vegetables rounds out a meal of spicy fajitas, beans, and tortillas. Green bell peppers can be substituted for red or yellow peppers.

Ingredients

2 medium red onions

*1 **each** medium red and yellow bell peppers and zucchini*

*1 **each** large Anaheim chile and fennel bulb*

1 small (about 1 lb.) eggplant

¼ cup olive oil

3 cloves garlic, crushed

Herb Dressing (see below)

Salt

Freshly ground pepper

Directions

1. Heat oven to 425°. Slice onions. Stem, seed, and quarter peppers and chile. Cut zucchini into ½-inch rounds. Trim fennel and cut into ½-inch wedges. Cut eggplant (peel, if desired) into ½-inch cubes.

2. In large shallow roasting pan, toss vegetables with olive oil and garlic. Bake, stirring often, until vegetables are well browned and eggplant is soft when pressed, about 40 minutes.

3. Let stand until vegetables are cool enough to handle. Pull off and discard skin from red and yellow peppers and chile. Cut in thin strips.

4. In large serving bowl, place vegetables and juices from roasting pan and toss with Herb Dressing. Season to taste with salt and pepper. Serve at room temperature or cover with foil and heat in oven, if desired.

Makes 4 servings

Herb Dressing

Ingredients

¼ cup balsamic or red wine vinegar

¼ cup chopped green onion, including green

1 teaspoon dried oregano leaves, crushed

Directions

Combine all ingredients.

Sweet Endings

Most southwestern desserts are sweet, satisfying, and substantial. They traditionally reflect the region's Mexican and Indian heritage, with custards, puddings, deep-fried pastries, and rich cookies. Today more of an emphasis is placed on fresh fruits and lighter offerings to end a full meal (Desert Ices, Grilled Fruit Skewers, Meringue Clouds with Fresh Fruit). Restaurants, too, have developed new, fanciful desserts that use regional flavors and images of the desert (Strawberry Margarita Pie). For a quick and easy finish, don't forget ice cream with a splash of Kahlúa (or make Kahlúa Frappés) as a great cooler for spicy-hot main dishes.

Strawberry Margarita Pie

A food processor crushes pretzels in no time. Use low-salt pretzels, if desired.

Ingredients

1¼ cups finely crushed pretzel crumbs

½ cup butter or margarine, melted

¼ cup sugar

¼ cup frozen pink lemonade concentrate, thawed

3 tablespoons tequila

2 tablespoons Triple Sec

1 tablespoon fresh lime juice

1 teaspoon grated lime peel

1 cup finely chopped strawberries

1 quart strawberry ice cream, softened

Sweetened whipped cream

Lime slices

Strawberries

Directions

1. In medium bowl, mix pretzel crumbs, butter or margarine, and sugar until well blended. Press mixture on bottom and up side of buttered 9-inch pie plate; chill.

2. In large bowl, mix lemonade, tequila, Triple Sec, lime juice, lime peel, and chopped strawberries. Stir in softened ice cream and mix well (work quickly).

3. Spoon mixture into chilled crust. Cover with plastic and freeze overnight. Serve wedges of pie garnished with dollops of whipped cream, lime slices, and/or strawberries.

Makes 1 9-inch pie

Desert Ices with Cinnamon Crisps

Freezing ices in a shallow pan speeds up the freezing process and makes it easier to break them up to puree. The cinnamon tortilla pieces remind me of pie dough scraps baked with cinnamon sugar.

Pineapple-Lemon Ice

Ingredients

1 cup water

¼ cup sugar

1 cup fresh pineapple chunks

*¼ cup **each** pineapple juice and lemon juice*

Cinnamon Crisps (see below)

Directions

1. In medium saucepan, combine water and sugar. Bring mixture to boil, stirring until sugar is dissolved; cool.
2. In food processor, purée pineapple. Blend in pineapple juice, lemon juice, and sugar syrup until well mixed.
3. Pour mixture into metal 13×9×2-inch baking pan. Cover and freeze until hard (at least 8 hours).
4. Break into small chunks and blend in food processor, using on/off bursts at first, then blending continuously until mixture is a smooth slush. Or, place in large bowl, break up, and beat with electric mixer.
5. Return slush to metal pan, cover, and freeze until firm, about 4 hours. Let stand at room temperature 10 minutes to soften slightly; serve with Cinnamon Crisps. Keeps frozen up to 1 month.

Orange-Rosemary Ice

Ingredients

1 cup water

¼ cup sugar

2 teaspoons finely chopped fresh rosemary leaves

1 teaspoon grated orange peel

2 cups fresh orange juice

Cinnamon Crisps (see below)

Directions

1. In medium saucepan, combine water, sugar, rosemary, and orange peel. Bring to boil. Cook until syrup is reduced to ⅔ cup; cool.
2. Stir orange juice into syrup. Proceed as in steps 3-5 above.

Makes 1 quart each

Cinnamon Crisps

Ingredients

Flour tortillas

Vegetable oil

⅓ cup sugar

1 teaspoon ground cinnamon

Directions

1. Cut tortillas into 2×¼-inch strips, or use small fancy cookie cutters to cut out shapes (stars, cactus, arrows, etc.).
2. In large deep skillet, heat ½ inch oil to 350°. In small bowl, combine sugar and cinnamon; set aside.
3. Fry tortilla strips or shapes 1 to 1½ minutes, until golden brown; drain on paper towels. Dredge in sugar-cinnamon mixture. Use to garnish ices or ice cream. Store airtight.

Banana Mousse Parfaits

This mousse can be prepared a day ahead, but wait to assemble the parfaits until just before serving or the Nut Crunch will get soggy.

Ingredients

Nut Crunch (see below)

1 lb. very ripe, fresh papaya or mango, or 1 can (16 oz.) apricot or peach halves in syrup, drained

2 medium (about ¾ lb.) very ripe bananas

¾ cup dairy sour cream

¼ cup packed brown sugar

2 tablespoons lime juice

1 cup whipped cream

Directions

1. Peel and seed papaya; cut into chunks. In food processor, purée papaya or mango, bananas, sour cream, brown sugar, and lime juice.

2. Pour fruit mixture in large bowl. Quickly fold whipped cream into mixture. Cover and refrigerate at least 2 hours (can be done 1 day ahead).

3. In each of 6 tall parfait glasses, layer fruit mousse and Nut Crunch two times, ending with Nut Crunch on top. Serve immediately.

Makes 6 servings

Nut Crunch

Ingredients

2 cups pecan halves

1 cup sugar

2 teaspoons ground cinnamon

Directions

1. Line baking sheet with aluminum foil.

2. In large heavy skillet, combine pecans, sugar, and cinnamon.

3. Cook over medium heat until sugar melts, stirring constantly.

4. Continue to cook and stir until sugar is a dark caramel brown and nuts are coated.

5. Pour mixture onto baking sheet and spread out. Cool and coarsely chop.

Kahlúa Frappés

The best way I can describe these frappés is to call them *adult* milkshakes!

Ingredients

1 cup milk

1 pint (2 cups) chocolate, vanilla, or coffee ice cream

½ cup coffee-flavored liqueur (Kahlúa)

Whipped cream

Chocolate-covered coffee beans or chocolate candy coffee beans (optional)

Directions

1. Pour milk into ice-cube tray and freeze until solid, about 4 hours. (Can be done ahead; once solid, cover or place cubes in recloseable plastic bag.)

2. In blender or food processor, combine frozen milk cubes, ice cream, and liqueur. Blend until smooth. Pour into chilled glasses and garnish with whipped cream and chocolate coffee beans, if desired.

Makes 3 servings

Grilled Fruit Skewers

As the grill cools down after you cook your entrée, throw on fresh fruit kabobs to finish off the meal. If you prefer, serve them with ice cream rather than sour cream sauce.

Ingredients

About 8 cups fresh fruit, cut into wedges or chunks (pineapple, mango, melon, pear, plum, nectarine, orange, and/or papaya)

Orange-flavored liqueur (optional)

Ground cinnamon (optional)

Superfine sugar (optional)

Orange Sour Cream Sauce (see below)

6 to 8 (12-inch) metal or bamboo skewers*

Directions

1. Thread fruit onto skewers. Place skewers on shallow platter and sprinkle with orange-flavored liqueur, if desired.

2. Place skewers on grill over medium coals until heated through and slightly browned, 4 to 6 minutes, turning often.

3. Serve immediately, sprinkled with cinnamon and sugar or with sauce.

*If using bamboo skewers, soak in water 20 minutes to prevent burning.

Makes 6 servings

Orange Sour Cream Sauce

Ingredients

16 oz. (2 cups) dairy sour cream

½ cup packed brown sugar

*2 tablespoons **each** orange juice and orange-flavored liqueur*

1 teaspoon grated orange peel

Directions

1. In small bowl, mix all ingredients.

2. Refrigerate.

Chocolate-Orange Flan

A variation of caramel custard, this chocolate-orange version incorporates two regional flavor favorites. If you'd like to bake the flan in one large dish, coat the bottom of a 1-quart, straight-sided baking dish with caramelized sugar. Pour in the custard mixture, place the dish in a water bath, and bake as directed. Garnish with orange slices.

Ingredients

1 cup sugar, divided

4 eggs

1¾ cups milk

2 tablespoons orange-flavored liqueur

3 oz. Mexican chocolate or semisweet chocolate, ground to fine powder in food processor

Directions

1. Heat oven to 325°. In small heavy saucepan, heat ½ cup sugar over medium heat, stirring gently, until it melts and turns golden brown. Pour immediately into bottoms of 6 (6-ounce) custard cups. Allow syrup to harden for 5 minutes.

2. In medium bowl, whisk eggs. Add milk, remaining ½ cup sugar, liqueur, and chocolate. Whisk until well blended.

3. Pour about ½ cup mixture into each custard cup. Place cups in 13×9×2-inch baking pan. Place in oven; fill pan with boiling water to depth of 1 inch.

4. Bake 50 minutes or until knife inserted near center of custards comes out clean. Remove cups from water bath. Cool custards on wire rack 15 minutes, then chill at least 2 hours.

5. To serve, carefully run tip of knife around edge of custards to release from cups. Unmold onto individual dessert plates.

Makes 6 servings

Sopaipillas (Soft Pillows)

This light, puffy fried dough is traditionally served either with honey as a dinner roll or dusted with powdered sugar as a dessert. Sometimes the sopaipillas are split and filled with cooked fruits. In New Mexico the dough is wrapped around savory fillings, then deep-fried like a turnover. Spooning the hot oil over the sopaipillas during frying is the secret to making them puff evenly.

Ingredients

2 cups all-purpose flour

2 teaspoons baking powder

½ teaspoon salt

2 tablespoons lard or vegetable shortening

¾ cup warm milk or water

Vegetable oil

Cinnamon sugar, powdered sugar, or honey

Directions

1. In large bowl, mix flour, baking powder, and salt. Cut lard or shortening into mixture with pastry blender or two knives until mixture resembles fine crumbs.

2. Gradually add milk or water; stir with fork until mixture forms dough. Knead dough on lightly floured surface just until smooth, about 2 minutes. Shape into ball; cover and let rest 20 minutes.

3. In Dutch oven, heat 1½ to 2 inches oil to 360°. On floured surface, roll dough into rectangle ¼ inch thick. Cut into 3×4-inch rectangles.

4. Fry, one or two at a time, until golden, about 2 minutes, spooning hot oil over tops to encourage even puffing. Drain on paper towels.

5. Serve sprinkled with cinnamon sugar, powdered sugar, or honey.

Makes about 16 sopaipillas

Rum Fruit Crisp

Vary the type of nuts you use in the crumble mixture—pecans, almonds, walnuts, or macadamias.

Ingredients

Nut Crumble (see below)

2 lbs. ripe pears, apples, mangoes, or pineapple

½ cup raisins (golden or dark)

*¼ cup **each** packed brown sugar, all-purpose flour, and rum*

3 tablespoons lemon juice

1 teaspoon grated lemon peel

Ice cream, whipped cream, or dairy sour cream

Directions

1. Heat oven to 400°. Grease 12×7×2-inch baking dish. Prepare Nut Crumble.

2. Peel, core, and thinly slice pears or apples, or peel mangoes or pineapple and cut into ½-inch pieces.

3. In large bowl, toss fruit with raisins, brown sugar, flour, rum, lemon juice, and lemon peel. Spoon mixture into prepared baking dish. Top with Crumble.

4. Bake until topping is well browned and filling is bubbling gently, 35 to 45 minutes. Serve warm with ice cream, whipped cream, or sour cream as desired.

Makes 8 to 10 servings

Nut Crumble

Ingredients

½ cup nuts

⅓ cup packed brown sugar

*½ cup **each** all-purpose flour and butter or margarine*

½ cup shredded coconut

Directions

1. In food processor, combine nuts and sugar. Process until well blended.

2. Add flour and butter or margarine. Process until well mixed.

3. Stir in coconut.

Meringue Clouds with Fresh Fruit

For a really fast dessert, fill meringues with ice cream and top them with butterscotch or hot fudge sauce.

Ingredients

3 large egg whites

¼ teaspoon cream of tartar

¾ cup sugar

Lemon yogurt or ice cream of choice

Fresh sliced fruit (strawberries, papaya, pineapple, and/or kiwi)

Directions

1. Heat oven to 275°. Line baking sheets with parchment paper.

2. In small mixing bowl, beat egg whites and cream of tartar at high speed until foamy. Gradually beat in sugar. Beat until stiff peaks form.

3. Drop meringue by ⅓ cupfuls onto parchment, 3 inches apart. Shape each mound into 3-inch circle with indentation in center.

4. Bake 1 hour. Turn off oven; leave meringues in oven with door closed 1 hour. Remove and finish cooling on wire rack. Store in airtight container if not using immediately.

5. To serve, fill Meringue Clouds with filling and fruits of choice.

Makes 8 to 10 servings

Cinnamon Meringue Clouds

Beat ½ teaspoon ground cinnamon into egg whites with sugar.

Aztec Caramel Pecan Brownies

These irresistible brownies can be made well ahead of serving. The Aztec Indians of Mexico first used unsweetened cocoa beans in cold beverages, but it was the Spanish explorers who took cocoa beans back to Europe and sweetened them.

Ingredients

Crust

2½ cups finely crushed pecan shortbread cookies

5 tablespoons butter or margarine, melted

Brownies

3 oz. (3 squares) unsweetened chocolate, chopped

¾ cup butter or margarine

1½ teaspoons vanilla extract

3 eggs

1¼ cups **each** packed brown sugar and all-purpose or unbleached flour

¾ cup chopped pecans

Filling

1 can (15 oz.) ready-to-spread coconut pecan frosting

Topping

1 oz. (1 square) unsweetened chocolate, chopped

¼ cup butter or margarine

¼ cup cream or milk

2½ cups powdered sugar

2 teaspoons rum extract or 1 tablespoon vanilla extract

Directions

1. Heat oven to 350°. Grease 13×9×2-inch baking pan. In small bowl, mix crushed cookies and melted butter or margarine. Press mixture into bottom of pan.

2. In medium saucepan, melt 3 oz. chocolate and ¾ cup butter or margarine over low heat, stirring constantly until smooth. Remove from heat.

3. Stir in 1½ teaspoons vanilla, eggs, and brown sugar; blend well. Stir in flour and pecans; mix well.

4. Spread mixture evenly over crust. Bake until set, 22 to 32 minutes. Cool.

5. Spread filling over cooled brownies. In small saucepan, combine 1 oz. chocolate, ¼ cup butter or margarine, and cream or milk over low heat, stirring constantly until smooth.

6. Remove from heat; stir in powdered sugar and extract until smooth. Pour over filling; spread to cover.

7. Refrigerate brownies for 30 minutes. Cut into bars. Store covered in refrigerator.

Makes 48 bars

Pine Nut Cookies

These melt-in-your-mouth cookies are similar to Mexican wedding cake cookies, which are made with pecans. Anise, a spice that tastes like licorice, is a popular flavoring for Mexican-style cookies.

Ingredients

½ cup butter or margarine, softened

1 cup plus 2 tablespoons powdered sugar, divided

2 teaspoons grated orange peel

1 teaspoon vanilla extract

1 cup whole wheat or unbleached flour

1 cup pine nuts, finely chopped*

½ teaspoon anise seed, crushed

⅛ teaspoon salt

Directions

1. Heat oven to 275°. In medium bowl, beat butter, 2 tablespoons powdered sugar, orange peel, and vanilla until creamy.

2. Stir in flour, nuts, anise, and salt until well mixed. Shape spoonfuls of dough into 1-inch balls. Place balls on ungreased baking sheet 1 inch apart, flattening slightly.

3. Bake until edges are light golden brown, 30 to 35 minutes.

4. Roll warm cookies in remaining 1 cup powdered sugar; cool. Roll in sugar again. Store airtight.

*Grinding nuts in food processor works well.

Makes about 4 dozen

Menu Ideas

Tex-Mex Fiesta

Nogales Popcorn Mix
Frozen Margaritas
Deluxe Fajitas
Warm Flour Tortillas
Borracho Beans
Pico de Gallo
Salsa con Tequila
Spanish Rice
Sonoran Guacamole
Grilled Fruit Skewers

Indian Summer Barbecue

Pork Fajitas in Red Chile Sauce
Warm Flour Tortillas
Chunky Guacamole
Spicy Black Beans with Goat Cheese
Cilantro and Red Pepper Slaw
Strawberry Margarita Pie

Mexico City Supper

Green Chile Dip
Tortilla Chips
Piña Coladas
Shrimp in Vera Cruz Salsa
Brown Rice with Cilantro and Pine Nuts
Jicama Julienne Salad
Banana Mousse Parfaits

Luncheon al Fresco

Zippy Pepita and Pine Nut Mix
Blushing Sangria
Topopo Salad Bowls
Salsa Roja
Orange-Rosemary or Pineapple-Lemon Ice
Cinnamon Crisps

Sonoran Dinner Party

Classic Nachos
Fajita Kabobs with Zucchini and Pineapple
Papaya Jicama Relish
Mexican Spiced Rice
Kahlúa Frappés

Harvest Supper

Sopa de Maíz (Corn Soup)
Chicken in Pumpkin Seed Sauce
Warm Tortillas
Acapulco Vegetable Ragout
Rum Fruit Crisp

Quick 'n Easy Do-Ahead Dinner

Guacamole with Vegetable Dippers
Tucson Cheese Crisps
Quick Black Bean Chili
Crisp Cucumber Salad
Fresh Fruit

Southwestern Picnic

Sweet Potato and Plantain Chips
Spicy Rosemary Lemonade
Citrus Tomato Gazpacho
Fajita Pockets
Black Bean Corn Salad
Aztec Caramel Pecan Brownies

New Year's Buffet

Antojitos Platter
Barbecued Chicken Fajita Enchiladas
Tomatillo Salsa
Rancho Refried Beans or Stewed Garbanzo Beans
Pine Nut Cookies

Summer Patio Supper

Orange-Honey Chicken Fajitas
Pineapple Citrus Relish
Grilled Vegetables
Garlic Roasted Potato Spears or Grilled Potato Packet
Chocolate-Orange Flan

Mail-Order Sources

Casados Farms
P.O. Box 1269
San Juan Pueblo, NM 87566
Dried chiles, corns, flours, spices, beans, and nuts.

The Chili Shop
109 E. Water St.
Santa Fe, NM 87501
(505) 983-6080
Condiments, seasoning blends, spices, salsas, fruit preserves, chile jellies, and flavored vinegars.

The Great Southwest Cuisine Catalog
Direct Marketing de Santa Fe
630 W. San Francisco
Santa Fe, NM 87501
(800) 872-8787, operator 46
(505) 982-5718
Wide assortment of salsas, chile sauces, blue corn products, condiments, masa harina, beans, seasoning blends, and marinades.

La Preferida
3400 W. 35th St.
Chicago, IL 60632
(312) 254-7200
Extensive line of canned chiles, Mexican vegetables, seasoning blends, herbs and spices, dried chiles, salsas, nuts, and flours.

Lazy Susan, Inc.
P.O. Box 10438
1702 S. Presa
San Antonio, TX 78210
(800) 972-3049 (outside Texas)
(800) 222-1537 (inside Texas)
Wait for tone and dial 994893 (for both numbers)
Salsas, seasoning blends, fajita seasoning, chili powder, and condiments.

Los Chileros de Nuevo Mexico
P.O. Box 6215
Santa Fe, NM 87502
(505) 471-6967
Packaged line of dried chiles, pure ground chile, pine nuts, corn husks, blue corn products, and other hard-to-find southwestern items.

Morgan's Mexican-Lebanese Foods
736 S. Robert St.
St. Paul, MN 55107
(612) 291-2955
A fully stocked Mexican market; write or call for mail-order information.

Pecos Valley Spice Co.
500 E. 77th St.
New York, NY 10162
(212) 628-5374
Dried ground chiles, herbs and spices, yellow and blue corn masa, dried corn husks, salsas, and chili spice mixes.

Santa Cruz Chile and Spice Co.
P.O. Box 177
Tumacocori, AZ 85640
Canned chiles, salsas and sauces, dried ground chile, and red chile paste.

For fresh red chiles for ristras (strings of chiles) and cooking (available in early fall):
My Santa Fe Connection
Box 1863
Corrales, NM 87048
(505) 842-9564

White Water Farms
Box 41
McNeal, AZ 85617
(602) 624-3624

True chile lovers can subscribe to a quarterly magazine devoted to the subject:
The Whole Chile Pepper
P.O. Box 4278
Albuquerque, NM 87196

Index